WLD

you've had a baby – now what?

A PRACTICAL GUIDE TO
FAMILY PSYCHOLOGY

Sold in the UK, Europe and Asia
by Faber & Faber Ltd,
Bloomsbury House,
74–77 Great Russell Street,
London WC1B 3DA
or their agents

Toronto,
Ontario M6J 2S1

Distributed in the USA
by Publishers Group West,
1700 Fourth Street,
Berkeley, CA 94710

Distributed in South Africa
by Jonathan Ball,
Office B4, The District,
41 Sir Lowry Road,
Woodstock 7925

ISBN: 978-178578-472-9

Typeset in Avenir by Marie Doherty

Printed and bound in Great Britain by Clays Ltd, Elcograf S.p.A.

About the author

James A. Powell, PsyD, is a clinical psychologist with over 47 years' experience working with real families and the problems they encounter. His methods have stood the test of time, come from sound theoretical principles and have been successfully used by thousands of families from all walks of life.

Dr Powell has an AA degree in psychology from Glendale College, a BA in psychology from Stanford University and his Doctor of Psychology (PsyD) from Baylor University. He has worked in psychiatric hospitals, mental health centres, school systems, probation departments, outpatient offices and the courts.

He has two grown children (of whom he is immensely proud), Clifton Powell and Eileen Sullivan. He currently resides in the UK with his wife of 44 years, Sherry, while working with the US Air Force.

To Sherry
You are the inspiration for all I do.

Contents

Introduction

Raising well-adjusted children in our complex society is an achievable goal. Almost all parents wish to do this and are anxious to do so in the best way possible. In my 42 years of practice as a psychologist I have worked with thousands of children and their parents to alleviate a host of problems such as lying, stealing, rebellion, temper tantrums, fears, anxieties and even self-mutilation. The purpose of this book is to share some of the experiences families have found most helpful and give parents extra support in managing their own children.

In today's society, families are often composed of single parents struggling to fulfil the role of mum and dad; parents from mixed races or ethnic groups; and grandparents who find themselves raising a second family. These situations each present their own challenges to the role of being a parent. While these differences are important, there are many common factors in child behaviour, whatever the make-up of the family. It is these characteristics that form the basis for many successful interventions in resolving problems.

The case studies in this book are drawn from my own experiences with children and the experiences of others, as well as valuable research studies. They are all real and involve actual families who sought help for their problems. All names or data that could specifically identify the individual or family have been deleted. The ways presented of dealing with these situations have all had success in real life. These are solutions that really work!

This book will help parents with children of different ages. Clinical practice has clearly indicated that a 'one size fits all' approach does not work: tots, under-tens, teens and adolescents all require different approaches.

Many, if not most, of the problems a parent encounters in raising a child in today's society can be dealt with successfully through a better understanding of the principles that create and aggravate problems. It is often the case that the solution which works best with a child involves the parents making changes in such things as their own attitudes, personal beliefs and actions. This book will help parents examine their own reactions to child behavioural difficulties, as well as offering an insight into the child's psyche.

When parents seek advice on improving their interactions with their children, they must keep four main concepts in mind:

• The child will often not perceive his or her behaviour in the same way as a parent.

• For each situation there are many choices for changing behaviour.

• Parents may do well to think back to their own childhood experiences.

- As children mature, their physiology and psychology are affected by biological influences.

Integrating these concepts into a successful approach to parenting is entirely possible for the typical parent and is key to raising children who are happy and well adjusted.

It is the purpose of this book to provide guidance, but if you find a situation to be unresolved after considering the suggested activities, then the assistance of a professional therapist can be invaluable. In such cases a parent will not be admitting defeat, but merely enlisting the support of someone with a wider knowledge of the 'behaviour battle'.

A note on style

While I began with the intention of keeping examples non-gender specific, I have had to modify this approach in a number of places to keep the text readable. In the majority of such cases I have adopted male pronouns but this is not intended to indicate any bias; unless stated otherwise, the situations described in this book are applicable to boys and girls alike.

1. Why have children?

Raising children is not as easy as having them. But it does not require a university degree, nor is it something that only a professional can do successfully. What is required is the perspective that the child is residing with you on a temporary basis and will soon be an adult. You have a responsibility to the child, to yourself and to society to try and teach them how to become a caring, respectful and responsible adult.

Perhaps the place to start in your quest to become the best parent possible is an examination of the reasons for having children in the first place.

'If I have his child he will see how much I love him'; 'I wanted something that was an expression of our love for each other'; 'We felt it was the right time to have children before we got too old to enjoy them'; 'I wanted something that was totally mine and that nobody could take away'; 'I love children and have always wanted a large family'; 'Having children just happened.'

All these reasons have been given in response to my query about why a person has had children. They tend to share a feature that is easily overlooked. This is that the child is viewed more as a possession than as a person. The child is referred to as though he or she exists only to satisfy a need of the parents rather than as an individual with his or her own unique desires, hopes and dreams.

Becoming a parent can be one of life's most precious moments. The joy of creating a new life, the satisfaction you feel from holding your child close, and the pride that one can have in a son or daughter are some of the most intense and satisfying feelings people can experience. However, it may be because of the very intensity of the love we have for our children that when disruptions occur in our relationship with them, we often feel bewildered, frustrated and confused. In coping with these reactions it is often beneficial to examine your own background for those influences that have shaped your perception of what is required to be a parent.

Children are, by their very nature, self-centred and demanding of more love, time and attention than they give. The perception that a child should automatically and unconditionally give the parent love and acceptance is an incorrect belief which often underlies the reactions we have to our children.

One example of not obtaining self-insight before becoming a parent is the situation where I was called upon to counsel a very pregnant thirteen-year-old girl referred to me by Social Services. She indicated that the session needed to end promptly at 11 o'clock because she had to get home and 'care for my children'. When I asked her about this she related that she had already given birth at age eleven and again at twelve, and that her own mother was caring for the children while she was seeing me.

'How does your mother feel about you having children so young?' I asked her. She said that her mother was fine with it because the father of the children, a former teacher, was a good man and both she and her mother believed that the more children she had with him, the more committed he would be to staying with her.

To this thirteen-year-old girl, having children was not only the product of her relationship with her lover but a way of ensuring his loyalty. Although she identified herself as a 'good mother', it was obvious that she had no concept of the enormity of the task she was assuming in creating and raising children.

Although this young girl probably did love her children, she lacked any real understanding of their developmental needs. She had not gone through the adolescent stages of separation and individuation herself, so how could she be expected to understand the role she had to play in raising kids?

It is necessary for parents to comprehend the developmental needs of children at their different ages if they are to succeed at parenting. This can be learned by almost all parents but first you must have the maturity that only time and experience can provide.

People are tempted to assume that the very unusual perspective on raising children displayed by the young girl was simply the result of physical immaturity. After all, she was just a child herself. Unfortunately, such attitudes are not limited to the young.

Consider a situation I experienced where a woman who was pregnant with her eighth child complained that Social Services had stolen all of her other brood shortly after their birth following accusations of neglect. Her stated plan was to continue to have children until Social Services tired of trying to find foster homes for them and then she would get all of her children back and would raise them the way she wished.

This woman was neither educationally disadvantaged nor seriously emotionally disturbed. Although she was somewhat extreme in going to the lengths of having so many children, her perception of parenting is tragically common. She believed that the *act of giving birth* was sufficient to instil in her the ability to raise a child. She was thinking of her own personal need to have something of her own, that would love her exclusively, and not of the needs of the youngster as a developing person. To simply love a child is not enough to raise a happy and well-adjusted person.

Perhaps such views were once acceptable but this is now long in our past. Our society has set various basic guidelines for the raising of children. As a parent, you must adequately feed, clothe, house and provide for the education of your children. Corporal punishment is restricted by the laws concerning abuse and neglect. Physical, sexual and emotional abuses are prohibited. Unfortunately, the definition of what is and is not abusive is often vague and unclear.

Most people would agree that screaming at a young person and calling them names (e.g. bitch, bastard, stupid, incompetent, ugly) is unacceptable at best and probably emotionally abusive. But what about telling your daughter that you wanted a son and not her? What happens when you tell your child that they don't have a father and that they should just be satisfied with you? Are these actions an attempt to be open and honest or are they emotional abuse? The answer requires an understanding of the developmental age and reasoning capabilities of your child, as well as your own motivations.

In the course of my practice over the past decades I have found that understanding your own reasons for having children in the first place is crucial in raising them to be happy. When this insight is combined with the age-appropriate capabilities of the child, parenting is not only much easier but can be a joyful experience. Self-awareness can help you become conscious of how attitudes and actions affect the problems children display and what *you* might have to do to change their behaviour.

It is important to remember that self-awareness does not necessarily mean self-blame. Very often parents will come to a psychologist with a feeling of guilt about their child's unmanageable outbursts or attitudes. They often feel it is their own fault that their son or daughter has a problem and that people will judge them as a bad parent because their child screams uncontrollably in public when denied a treat or toy. Parents need to remember that children are not born as a blank slate upon which we can write and determine the formula of their psychology.

REMEMBER THIS!!! Children are born with inherent tendencies that are moulded by their environment, nutrition and the way others, including parents, react to them. Thus while parents may believe that they can create desirable qualities, the reality is that they can influence only a part of the developmental process. Basic qualities that were once thought to have developed entirely through the child's interactions with others, such as shyness, in fact tend to have a strong genetic component. For example, researchers at the University of Colorado and Pennsylvania State University observing identical and fraternal twins have indicated that genetics constitutes roughly half of the underpinning of shyness.

This does not mean that the difficulties parents have should simply be accepted as part of the child's inherent nature. Parents should not assume the total blame for a youngster's actions but should assume the responsibility to change or moderate concerning behaviours.

There are many and various things that a parent may try. With the correct approach, clear improvements in behaviour can occur, even if the problem does not disappear entirely. Parents can apply the activities suggested in the following chapters to produce someone that can be the source of pride and enjoyment that was hoped for when first conceived. The satisfaction that comes from raising a well-behaved child is one true source of riches that can and should be yours.

2. And Then There Were Three

Generally there are five ways that a child comes into a family:

- Planned-for event.
- Happy (or not so happy) surprise.
- After infertility treatment.
- Adoption.
- Through inheritance from another family member.

Each of these pathways into the family brings with it unique but similar challenges. Therapists have found that couples traditionally fight about three things the most: money, sex and children. It can be reasonably argued that children significantly affect the first two of the three.

If the addition was a planned or hoped-for event then the parents are perhaps better able to accept the deprivations that will occur when their child arrives. They have decided that enlarging the family is a joint goal, so when they have to limit their outside activities in order to care for the baby, they can at least rationalize that this was something they chose. Parents may still not like the loss of freedom, nor the expense of it all, but they can usually accept it.

In the situation where the child was not planned, the 'surprise' can be either happy or devastating. If both parents are agreeable that enlarging the family is both desirable and timely then the result can be the same as if this was a planned event. Unfortunately, there is often one parent who is more distressed by the pregnancy than the other. Resentment and accusations are typical responses to an unplanned pregnancy, with much bemoaning of the costs involved and the 'poor timing' of the event. Anger can escalate to the point of breaking up a relationship, or in some cases a rush to get married when the couple are not really ready for such a level of commitment.

 The key to coping with an unplanned pregnancy is talking with your significant other in an open and honest manner. Try to keep fears associated with becoming a mum or dad in perspective, for these are experienced by most new parents. Is there ever a time when we are truly ready to add a child to our lives? Do we ever have enough money saved to raise a son or daughter? Most parents would resoundingly respond 'no' to these questions and yet they still manage to raise healthy and happy children. You can too, if you are willing to confront your fears and share them with your partner. Together, as a team, you can conquer your worries and make up for any real or imagined deficiencies as a parent.

Infertility treatments carry their own special baggage in addition to the typical concerns that surround having a baby. There is a very high expectation of becoming pregnant that is often followed by repeated disappointment. Sexual interactions can become a chore due to the need to perform on demand at the whim of a device that indicates ovulation. This change in attitude towards having sex can last long after a baby is conceived.

'Sex on demand' sounds like something associated with a prostitute. Yet this is essentially what is required, regardless of your mood, when ovulation is anticipated. If you can learn to laugh with your partner at your state of affairs and see the humour in what you are doing, then most resentments evaporate. What is a temporary inconvenience can become a charming intimate anecdote as your lives together progress.

When a couple reaches the decision to adopt it is typically after a very frustrating period of trying to conceive. Most people find the adoption process to be abysmally long and expensive. The number of infants available is low compared to demand. The decision to adopt brings you into confrontation with personal racial biases, preferences as to gender and age, and even the possibility of taking on someone with special needs.

In addition, the adoptive couple today often has to confront the possibility of sharing their family with the biological parents. The American Association of Open Adoption

Agencies defines an 'open adoption' as 'a form of adoption in which the birth family and the adopted child enjoy an ongoing, in-person relationship'. In 1975, on moral grounds, both England and Wales passed laws allowing every adopted individual access to their birth records. The UK Office for National Statistics has projected that 33 per cent of all adoptees eventually request a copy of their original birth records, although studies suggest this may be a somewhat low number. These concerns can sorely test the stability and coherence of an adoptive couple, even to the point of breaking up.

USEFUL TIP

You have love which together you want to give to a new member of your relationship. You are creating a family. Although the journey to adopt can be arduous, it does have an end point. When this is reached, the vast majority of people find that the result was well worth the effort.

In our current society an increasing number of births are to single females who may be emotionally unprepared to become a parent but who have chosen not to have an abortion. Instead, some go down the route of seeking a relative to adopt the baby. Raising a child born to another family member has many of the concerns of adopting but with the added complexity of extended family members knowing that the birth parents are other relatives. There is often the fear that the biological mother or father may want to reassert their 'rights' at some point. This concern is like a ticking time bomb to many couples and it takes extraordinary emotional strength and flexibility to cope with this fear so that it does not erode the bond between the parents.

 The old saying that 'an ounce of prevention is worth a pound of cure' is correct. Rather than fret about whether the biological parents will intervene in your lives, make your views and desires crystal clear at the time you assume responsibility for the youngster. State your needs about what others can say and do around *your* child to all family members. Then write this down so that you, and they, will know exactly what is expected.

Regardless of the mode by which a couple becomes a family, few people are truly prepared for the impact the addition will have on their attitudes and interactions with their partner. If you ask a person who has never had children what it would be like to become a parent, they will typically give a glowing description of their hopes and dreams for their son or daughter. Most descriptions are centred on the joys of raising a child, the sense of completion they would experience and the activities involved in helping them to be happy and successful. Many times they will talk about their own childhoods and use this as a reference, either as something to aspire to or to avoid. Both partners usually agree upon these general ideals. However, it is in the nitty-gritty of the actual parenting that difficulties may arise.

Consider these three essential hardships involved in creating a family:

- Emotional.
- Physical.
- Financial.

Sexual relationships between partners are impacted by the need to spend time feeding, changing, washing and dressing a new addition. Loss of sleep is almost inevitable. Who really enjoys getting up three times a night with a crying baby? With exhaustion often comes a reassessment of personal priorities. The partner who goes to an outside job insists that they *must* get some rest and justifies this by thinking, and sometimes saying, that childcare is the responsibility of the stay-at-home partner since now they 'do not really work'. Sleep may become more important than making love. The routine of putting a child to bed can be time-consuming and at times frustrating.

Studies suggest that 10–15 per cent of women after giving birth develop Postnatal Depression (PND). This particular syndrome often gives rise to irritability, anxiety, a loss of sleep and exhaustion. The loss of sexual desire in depressed individuals is significant. This condition may last for many months after birth and severely impact the relationship between partners.

The costs of such things as nappies, prams and new clothes come as a shock to many people. Trips to the pub may be curtailed by the need to pay for these items and at times it often appears that parents are doing nothing else but working and caring for their offspring. Personal time and space are often gone, or if maintained by one then resented by the caregiving parent who remains home.

As the little one ages there comes the need to decide when to have a new baby. Most parents want two or more children and begin to worry about the age difference. They fret that if their children are too far apart in age they will not play with each other. They also become concerned about being too old to have further children. All of these things can easily lead to disagreements.

These differences are resolvable but they require patience and understanding on the part of both partners. When you are discussing having an addition to the family it is necessary to go beyond the generalities and talk about the daily impact upon your lifestyles:

- How will you cope with the loss of income?

- Which partner is going to a job and which will stay home?

- Will the grandparents be used as babysitters?

- Do you want to raise a family in the city or the country?

- What is 'spoiling' a child or babying and what is not?

The list goes on and at times seems almost endless.

It is not necessary to answer all of these questions before you move forward with a family. However, it is important to establish a framework for responding to the inevitable differences between the two of you that the process of raising children brings to light.

The key concepts here are:

- A sense of being in it together.
- Respect for the other person.
- Compromise.
- The ability to take a long-term perspective.

You and your partner are a team who have taken on one of the most important tasks in the world together. Both of you have valuable insights and opinions with regard to rearing children, even if you are not aware of them.

A good example is the question of how long you breastfeed your child. A woman who especially enjoys babies may want to continue breastfeeding up to age three or more. However, her partner may look forward to the child maturing into a person he can introduce to sports or another favourite pastime, and he may see this prolonged breastfeeding as delaying the child's development. He may vent his unhappiness in directives to 'Stop babying him!', which in turn might be perceived as insensitive to the needs of the mother and child. Neither parent is 'right' or 'wrong' in this situation. Discussing your goals and expectations can usually result in finding common ground and prevent many hurt feelings.

You must remind yourselves constantly that childrearing is a phase that will eventually end when your independent son or daughter moves out and then it will be just the two of you again. If you have maintained the respect and love of your partner throughout the process then the next phase of life can be as enjoyable and fulfilling as that which came before.

3. The Day After

By sticking it out through tough times, people emerge from adversity with a stronger sense of efficacy.

—Albert Bandura, *Encyclopedia of Human Behavior*, 1994

Once the family has been formed, the reality of the joys and stresses of raising a child begins. Watching a baby's first steps, hearing his or her first words, and the pride of being referred to as 'mum' or 'dad' are priceless. However, there are still important issues that need to be addressed:

- Spending time with your child.
- Giving the primary caregiver a break.
- Keeping on top of housework.
- Making time for each other as a couple.

Too often these are the points of contention that cause arguments and hurt feelings unless the partners address them quickly.

Typically one parent continues to work while the other stays home with the new baby, and the 'working' partner may become critical of the stay-at-home mum or dad when the hoovering is not done as frequently as before or the dishes are piling up in the kitchen. Conversely, the stay-at-home parent perceives the working partner as being unaware of all the time-consuming activities that are needed to care for an infant. Arguments easily occur when the partner with an outside job asserts his or her need to rest when at home because, after all, *they* have worked all day.

 Resentments can be prevented if both of you are sensitive to the needs of the other and remember that you are equally important to the functioning of your family. The old adage that 'you can't sink only one half of a ship' is well worth remembering.

How much time should the working partner spend with the child at night? The answer to this is complex and varies with the individual needs of both partners. There is no set or simple answer. A child needs time with both parents from birth onwards. Each parent should recognize their own need for contact with their son or daughter, as well as the child's needs. Play time is extremely important for bonding.

Professor Michael D. Resnick of the University of Minnesota, and his associates, in a report on findings from the United States National Longitudinal Study on Adolescent Health in 1997, compared adolescents whose parents were often absent throughout the day with peers whose parents were present when they went to bed, woke up and came home from school. The youths whose parents were around them were found to be less likely to experience emotional distress. There was also a significant decrease in the likelihood of emotional distress if they engaged in activities with their parents.

Just as important as time spent with children is the time you spend with your partner. Before you became a family you were a couple. Hopefully, long after your children are grown you will still be a couple. This does not occur without effort. It is critical that parents still see themselves as a couple – and as individuals – even while raising children. The little endearments that you gave to your partner when it was just the two of you – the compliments, the smiles and touches, the loving kisses – and likewise the sexual relationship, are just as important when you become a parent as they were before your child came into the family.

Parents should make time for themselves without guilt. When you do so you are setting the model for your children to emulate as they mature and move on to their own parenthood. Becoming a parent should be viewed as a joyous shared adventure and not as a burden or an ending of the previous relationship.

Even when you have achieved the balance in your lives between being parents and partners, and have agreed upon many of the guidelines for childrearing, children can develop behavioural or emotional problems. The following chapters will address a number of these difficulties and suggest remedies that many families have found to be helpful. If there is one thing that decades of therapeutic practice have demonstrated clearly it is that there is always an answer to every problem. Remain hopeful, persevere, and with love and understanding almost everything can be overcome.

4. Attack of the Wild Things

Parents who are afraid to put their foot down usually have children who step on their toes.

—Chinese proverb

 Her son was three and at first appeared to be well behaved. He played quietly on the floor of my office as the mother explained that she was fearful that there was something terribly wrong with him because when frustrated he would often bite himself or others. At times he would scream uncontrollably and had recently progressed to banging his head against the floor, walls, doors and any other convenient object.

As we talked he became bored with the toys that I had set out and went over to a wall next to my desk to explore a computer outlet with various cables coming out of it. His mother became anxious and stated in a firm voice, 'No Jeremy!' which was completely ignored. As he began to pull on the cables her voice rose by several decibels and she again stated very emphatically, 'No Jeremy!' but was again ignored.

By this time he had pulled one of the cables out of the wall and in desperation she screamed, 'Jeremy, I said no! Don't touch that!' while still remaining on the couch just out of the reach of the child. The next actions by Jeremy were dramatic and swift. He screamed an ear-piercing shriek, threw himself on the floor, bit his hand and rolled around crying and kicking at anything and everything in his way. By this stage the mother was in tears, obviously embarrassed, and had gathered him up in her arms (thus receiving several kicks to her leg and side as she did so). She tried to soothe him, saying in a soft voice, 'It's okay Jeremy. Did you hurt yourself? Let me see your hand. Let mum kiss it and make it all better. It's okay. Mummy loves you.'

While she was soothing her son she was rocking him back and forth on her lap. Gradually the screaming and sobs subsided until eventually he had calmed down and she gently let him move off her lap and onto the floor. Jeremy gave his mum a defiant look, kicked her shin and started off towards the cables again. The mother's demeanour changed once again and she screamed, 'No Jeremy! I said no! Don't touch that!'

In response to this he ran across my room, selected a spot and whacked his head against the solid wall with an audible 'thunk'. The result was another round of blood-curdling screams to the point that the receptionist several offices away phoned to see if everything was all right. By this point the mother was sobbing uncontrollably and had gathered Jeremy once again in her arms. She was rocking him on the couch while making soothing sounds. She kissed his head and reassured him that mummy loved him and everything would be okay. Jeremy continued to kick and hit at her and everything within reach. The mother then plead-ingly asked me, 'Do you think it's a brain tumour?'

Therapists have had similar scenarios played out countless times in their offices and the answer to her question is 'No, we do not think that the cause is a brain tumour.' Parents have sought help when concerned that there is something genetically/physically wrong with their child or that he or she must be possessed. Parents have gone to the point of consulting a priest for a possible blessing. However, it is neither demonic possession nor genetic problems that have caused the temper tantrums. Instead the cause is something that child psychologists have dealt with for decades and is referred to as 'inappropriate reinforcement'.

'Reinforcement theory' or 'operant conditioning' is a fairly simple concept but has rather unusual implications in the context of parenting. Anything that increases the likeli-hood of an outcome occurring may be considered a 'posi-tive reinforcer' and anything that decreases the prospect may be characterized as a 'negative consequence'.

For a young child, positive reinforcers may be hugs, kisses, attention, stroking, soothing statements of love, food, toys, etc. The child wants these things, so will behave in the way most likely to earn them. Negative consequences may be the taking away of any of these things as well as smacking, harsh statements or shouting, etc. It is important to understand that things which may seem to be negative to the parent may be perceived by the child as positive.

This is often the case where the 'negative' is sending the child to their room, which to the child is a positive place full of toys and games.

When parents want a child to repeat the behaviour of putting toys away they might squeal with delight when he does and give him a hug with a verbal cue such as 'Good boy!' If parents want him to stop doing something then often they will yell 'No! Don't do that!'

Most of us intuitively recognize this from our own upbringings and the reactions of society to our behaviour. Our entire legal system, when broken down to its basics, is based on these simple principles.

What, then, has gone so terribly wrong that a child has developed what almost everybody would recognize as intolerable behaviour that no sane person would want to reward or encourage? The answer is that probably the parent has given a response that was either inappropriate or was at the wrong time.

In the case study of Jeremy, the mother at some time in the past encouraged curiosity and exploratory behaviour. After all, we want our children to be independent and to learn about the world around them.

As Jeremy learned to walk, talk and play with toys, his mum and dad had given him the usual praise and hugs, thus encouraging these exploratory behaviours. Then of course Jeremy had done something that was considered undesirable or bad, such as pulling the cat's tail, resulting in his being scratched and crying in pain.

Almost all parents hate to see their child in pain and typically will rush to reassure him that they will make the hurt better. They will kiss and cuddle while at the same time telling him, usually in a mild or soothing voice, something like 'Oh what a naughty cat! Now, now, Jeremy, you shouldn't pull the cat's tail. It isn't nice, it hurts the kitty and you can be hurt too!' This is almost a natural instinct but it can start a child down a path that can lead to the development of severe temper tantrums. The parents have unconsciously given very confusing messages to the child.

On the one hand, the parent has given him the same sorts of positive reinforcers that were used in the past to encourage good behaviour (e.g. hugs, kisses, a soothing voice) and inadvertently associated it with something that is to be discouraged (i.e. pulling the cat's tail). The adult believes that they have clearly separated out the two by stating that the child has engaged in an undesirable or dangerous activity. In reality, this is clear only in the parent's mind and not the child's.

How many of us have seen such an activity occur and then afterwards observed the now-comforted child stamp his foot in anger towards the cat while saying 'Bad kitty!', causing the cat to jump away? The next parental response is crucial because the child at this point believes that the problem lies in the *cat* being bad and not in him. Parents are often so relieved to see their child safe that they release their anxiety in laughter. The result is that the child becomes confirmed in the idea that the object (in this case the cat) was the problem and not his own actions.

He is quite likely to blame the cat again when he pulls its tail because he was inappropriately reinforced by the laughter of the parent. However, if when he stamps his foot at the cat we tell him, in a firm, negative voice, 'No Jeremy! The cat was not bad. You pulled his tail and hurt him. We don't hurt animals. We treat them gently', then you have given a negative response to the idea of hurting animals by your tone of voice.

The mother of Jeremy tried to stop her son's misbehaviour by shouting. However, any effect that this had was quickly overwhelmed by the potent positive reinforcers of holding him in her lap, rocking him, kissing him, etc. The mixed messages received by Jeremy resulted in frustration with him then striking out at his mother and ultimately banging his head. This 'bad' behaviour was then followed by inadvertent reinforcement of his self-harm by the mother holding and rocking him once again. This unfortunate cycle tended to repeat itself endlessly.

 The key to eliminating most problems is a comprehensive understanding of the step-by-step actions you have taken with your child. You must learn what is reinforcing to him and what is not. The next step is to have a clear idea in your own mind of what is acceptable and unacceptable behaviour. If you then apply the negatives to only those behaviours you wish to eliminate, and the positives to only those you wish to encourage, temper tantrums tend to rapidly decrease in intensity and frequency.

This seems fairly clear and straightforward with young children, and parents can readily appreciate this distinction with some practice. The situation with older children and adolescents tends to be a bit more complex, although the same principles apply and often we make the same mistakes.

CASE STUDY Let's say that our school-age son has ridden his bicycle out into the road down a hill that we have repeatedly told him not to go down. He has skidded on loose gravel, had an accident (foreseen by the parent) and now comes to us with a grazed leg full of gravel bits. As the parent picks out the gravel to painful cries, the parent will often scold the child for doing what he was told not to do. At one and the same time the parent wants to reassure the child that the leg will be better and will make soothing statements to try and comfort him. Confused messages have once again been given.

To avoid the mixed messages, the parent must clearly differentiate what it is that they are really trying to show or say to the child. When a child is hurt, the first order of business is to comfort and administer first aid. Only *after* the child's physical injury has been treated and he is calm do we then explain that the very reason why he had been forbidden to ride his bicycle down the hill was because of the foreseeable accident. When this has been done the parent must impose consequences for the child's disobedience. One appropriate negative action might be to take away the privilege of riding the bike for the next day. It is the timing and separation of the communications to the child that is critical.

This is especially true with older children, who tend to be very impulsive. Many parents find this difficult because when our own emotions are hot we feel like there is a need to respond immediately to remedy the situation. Taking the time to reflect on the proper sequence of actions is almost always well worth the wait.

Prevention is of course always best but if a negative pattern of behaviour has been established it does not mean that all is lost. Behaviour modification approaches have been developed which are often very successful in changing reactions. As part of such an approach it is necessary for the parents to first understand how their responses have helped to create the problem and then to change their pattern so that they no longer give mixed messages. Comforting and rewarding actions need to be clearly distinguished and separated from chastisement or the use of negatives.

A significant concern for many parents surrounds the use of negatives towards their children. Parents worry that they might smack a child too hard, or perhaps if they are taking some privilege away that they are doing so for too long or too short a time. These concerns are legitimate, for often 'punishment' only suppresses behaviour and does not correct the underlying attitude of the child. However, there is a well-tried technique that has been developed for delivering negative consequences in a way that avoids this problem. Parents may use a response known as 'time-out' where the child is not allowed to do fun things for a short time.

The concept of using time-out for your son or daughter is based on the idea that boredom is negative for people of all ages. Humans crave stimulation. Therefore when a time-out is given to a child, the idea is to put them in a setting in which there is basically nothing for them to do. The setting could be in a corner, in a chair or at a table, where they must sit quietly. In such a setting they are not allowed to do such fun things as read, listen to music, talk with others, play with toys or watch TV. The setting should not be scary or uncomfortable but simply uninteresting. Thus sending someone to their bedroom is *not* really a time-out for a child.

The amount of time that your youngster stays in time-out should be brief and is typically one minute for each year of age. While in the time-out setting the child must be quiet; thus the timing of being in the setting should be re-started if they cry, fuss or yell out. The reinforcement or 'positive' for the good behaviour of sitting quietly is the opportunity to return to their usual environment and activities, and to be around other people.

This is a way of demonstrating clearly that the misbehaviour is undesirable. This action, plus avoidance of any mixed messages, will gradually clarify for the child what the parent believes to be undesirable. It should also begin to decrease the frequency of outbursts, dangerous behaviour, and so on.

If another adult comes along and responds by shouting or trying to cajole the young person out of the tantrum, the efforts will be thwarted and the outbursts are likely to continue unabated. Inconsistency between parents often makes misbehaviour much more difficult to change. This fact is due to the child being exposed again to contradictory messages of correct and incorrect behaviour. Consistency among parents, grandparents and other carers is crucial in eliminating temper tantrums.

 While these actions are usually successful in eliminating meltdowns they must be maintained and expanded upon if further undesirable behaviour is to be avoided. The old adage that 'nature hates a vacuum' is true. After eliminating the basic tantrum it is necessary to teach your child what you want them to do in place of the bad behaviour. For the younger child this may involve direct explanations or role-modelling of what you want them to do in a situation. With the older child or adolescent it is best if you guide *them* into stating what would have been the better action to have taken. If the youth appears to have originated the 'better action' and describes it in their own words then it is much more likely that he or she will display this the next time a similar situation occurs.

Working with adolescents

Changing basic attitudes and behaviour is much easier and more rewarding for you and your child the earlier you start. In teenagers, temper tantrums tend to evolve into rebellion and defiance, often characterized by their engaging in dangerous and risky behaviours such as shoplifting, joyriding, unprotected sex and so on. Nevertheless, if you are the parent of a teenager you do not need to despair, for the techniques used with younger children can still be effective in changing your teen's behaviour if you add the additional component of reason.

As adolescents mature, they develop the reasoning powers and argumentative skills of adults. If you simply dole out consequences without explanations then you will appear arbitrary and tyrannical. Although the typical adolescent will not tell you that he or she accepts your reasons for imposing a punishment, they will internally value the fact that you have given an explanation.

 When you offer a justification for your reactions to bad or anti-social behaviour, you are helping your teenager to develop the reasoning powers of an adult. You are demonstrating the importance of looking at different sides of an issue instead of just the one way that is so characteristic of adolescence. This opportunity to help them develop into a reasoning adult should not be wasted.

Responses by harassed parents such as 'Because I am the boss and I say so!' need to be avoided. Adults know how infuriating this is to hear from a superior at work and to an adolescent it is just as frustrating and irritating. You must try to role-model even-handedness, compassion and impartiality.

Parents need to remember that what they are trying to instil in their children is the trait of self-discipline. In our anger at having been defied or at a display of anti-social behaviour we tend to lash out and to hurt (either physically or emotionally) so that our child will 'learn a lesson'. Thus many parents feel that the consequences they have given are not severe enough if the child is not crying or hurting. This is nonsense. The goal of parenting is to teach self-regulation and the infliction of suffering is at best a waste of time and at worst counterproductive. It is the process and framework of responding to what we perceive as being right or wrong that is the important lesson we are teaching. If this concept underlies our responses then self-regulation is much more likely to develop.

5. Liar, Liar, Pants on Fire!

If you tell the truth, you don't have to remember anything.
—Mark Twain

'You can't believe anything that comes out of his mouth! He will lie about everything, even when there's no need. He knows that I can't stand a liar and I punish him more for that than whatever it was he did wrong in the first place!'

I have heard such proclamations from many parents and they tend to be genuinely puzzled by the failure of their child to understand that 'honesty is the best policy'. Actions by parents to eliminate lying typically involve the use of responses designed to 'teach a lesson they won't forget', such as smacking, lecturing or depriving the child of toys and treats. Older children may find themselves grounded or have restrictions imposed on their favourite activities. Such parental responses are rarely effective in changing the behaviour.

By the time the parent has decided to seek help from a counsellor, the lying is usually very pervasive and has often gone on for many months, if not years. Changing such prevalent behaviour, whatever the age, is neither easy nor quickly accomplished. On the other hand the situation is never really hopeless.

The first thing parents should do is list the most important areas or activities in which untruthfulness occurs.

Usually this generates a list of perhaps five or six items such as brushing teeth, doing schoolwork, completing chores and feeding pets. Most parents are surprised at this because the lying is so frustrating that they tend to believe that it is everywhere and encompasses everything that a child does. Rarely do you find that the problem is as far reaching as the parent believes.

The next activity for the parent is to recognize and list positives about the child:

- Do they ever say that they love you?

- Have they ever done things that make you proud?

- Have they ever done tasks that you have asked them to do?

Almost always the answer to such questions is yes. The parent then begins to appreciate that their perceptions have been warped by the current difficulty.

What, then, has gone wrong to transform your child from one who is truthful to one who lies about doing simple tasks that could be completed in just a few minutes? Why does he or she expend huge amounts of energy in creating often elaborate stories (i.e. lies) about why they have not done something instead of just doing it? The answer is simple and yet profound. Lying has worked for the child in the past, in the sense that a lie has been successful in helping avoid work and/or trouble.

Parents often feel that when they are lied to it is a personal affront. The parents believe that somehow their son or daughter has become untrustworthy and betrayed them. After all, haven't they always emphasized truthfulness? The conclusion often reached is that someone must have placed this concept of lying into their child's head, for it does not reflect the parents' own beliefs and values. This is an unfortunate misinterpretation of the situation.

For a parent to correctly understand the origins of untruthfulness they must appreciate that a young person does not think the same way as an adult. This is somewhat difficult to comprehend, for we tend to believe that the way we think now is the way we have always reasoned, and the only thing that has changed is that we are older and more experienced.

Jean Piaget (1896–1980) was a biologist who later in life moved into the study of the cognitive development of children. His major discernments concern how children change over time in their ability to understand and respond to the world. Children cannot do certain types of thinking until they are psychologically mature enough, and this tends to occur at fairly consistent ages.

Here is a simple experiment that parents with a youngster under the age of seven can do, which helps understand the child's reasoning. It is an example of the concept referred to as 'conservation of matter'.

43

Put your child on one side of a table with you sitting opposite. Place three items on the table: a clear jug of water and two glasses of equal capacity, one tall and narrow, the other short and wide.

Tell the child to watch closely while you half fill the short, wide glass. Then take the short, wide glass and pour the water into the tall, narrow glass. Then take the jug and pour the same amount of water into the short glass again. Now ask a simple question: Which glass has the most water in it?

Adult reason would dictate that since we filled the tall glass from the short glass and then refilled the short glass to the same level, the two glasses must hold the same amount of water. Almost always, the youth under about age seven will say that the tall, narrow glass holds more water. This is not due to faulty learning, inexperience or lack of cognitive skills. It is due to the fact that children's minds do not function in the same way as those of adults.

When a child reaches around age seven, the physical maturity of the brain has developed to a point where adult reasoning to such problems becomes possible. Before this, the 'immature' reasoning is that the taller glass will have more water simply because it is taller.

After performing this experiment, many parents will lecture their young children on their faulty thinking, explaining why the glasses contain the same amount of water, sometimes making their point quite forcefully. When the parent is no longer present, the young person will usually revert back to a belief that the taller glass holds more water.

 If you accept the fact that youngsters do not reason in the same way as adults over such a simple thing as the amount of water in a glass, then how can you expect them to reason in an adult way about an infinitely more involved concept such as being truthful? The obvious answer is that children do not think about truthfulness and lying in the same way that adults do.

Parents often assume that a child who responds untruthfully has betrayed the parental trust. In reality, 'lying' is an adult concept that is best applied only to adolescents and other adults.

This does not mean that we should give up on teaching moral values to our children. Positive moral instruction is an important basic part of parenthood and should begin from the earliest ages. Your reaction to a child you believe is not being truthful should be based on the aim of helping them grow into an adult with well-balanced morals and ethics. You should not assume that they have already acquired these concepts and are just deliberately defying you.

After making this cognitive shift in your own thinking, much of the resentment and upset caused by lying should disappear. You then can recognize that what you have in front of you is a teaching opportunity.

Most children want to receive the praise and attention of adults around them. Thus saying something which may result in such praise, even if what they say is not really true (i.e. is a 'lie' to the adult), makes perfect sense.

This does not mean that you have to accept a lack of truthfulness in your youngster and just put up with lies. Instead it means that you have to teach that they will be rewarded for *telling the truth* (for example that he or she did not do the assignment or feed the dog) as opposed to responding with what they think you want to hear.

Imagine a situation where you ask your child if he has cleaned up his room. He may have done some of the things that you expected but not all. In the child's mind he wants you to feel good about his actions and thus it is easiest to simply say 'yes'. In this half-truth situation, is the child really lying or is he telling the 'truth'? Most situations with young children are of this nature, in that there is not a clear answer. When a parent suspects that their child has not done all of the tasks they were told to do, questioning of exactly what *has* been accomplished usually follows.

When your child admits to not doing everything, the usual reaction is hurt that you have been 'lied' to. However, if instead of getting angry you compliment the child on what he has accomplished, point out that you are proud of him for *telling* you about the things he has and *has not* completed and then patiently explain what else he needs to do to finish the chore, then everybody wins. In this way you are training him to reply honestly to your query and thus you have turned a potentially negative situation into a teaching opportunity.

Certainly the task itself is important and a child must learn to complete it. Yet trying to shame him into doing the task by shouting or labelling him as lazy or devious is rarely effective and usually counterproductive. One common pitfall encountered by parents as they attempt to grasp this change is that they will unconsciously set their children up to lie. It is important that you become aware of how this can happen and learn to avoid this result.

A parent who knows the answer to a question before it is asked can structure the approach in several different ways. You might say any of the following to your child, in the knowledge that the truthful answer is 'no':

- 'Did you do all of your school assignment?'

- 'Have you done the dishes?'

- 'Did you come straight home from the cinema?'

In reality, you know that the assignment has not been done because you spoke to another parent from your child's class and she remarked on that evening's over-long project. Similarly, you may have seen the dirty dishes in the sink when you came into the house, and a friend may have told you earlier that your child was at their house for most of the afternoon and therefore clearly did not come straight home from the cinema. By asking the child a *question* most parents feel they are giving the child a chance to be 'honest' about his or her behaviour. In reality, however, you are setting him up to lie.

A much more effective approach would be to say something like, 'I noticed the dirty dishes were still in the sink as I came in. You were told to do them after you came home. Do you want to wash them now or after dinner?' For the situation where they went to a friend's house instead of coming straight home you could say, 'I was told by John's mum that you were over at her house all afternoon. You disobeyed my instructions to come straight home. We need to talk about what you should and should not have done.' Regarding the assignment you could say something like, 'I know that your project will take a long time to do tonight and could not be completed by the time I came home. Do you need me to help you work on it now or after we eat dinner?'

In all of these situations you are setting your child up to tell you the truth and simultaneously to think about solutions to problems. They will see you as somebody who is 'on their side' and not just somebody to please out of a fear of being punished.

Does this mean that when your child does not do as you have requested that you just ignore it? Absolutely not. When the assignment is not done, chores are ignored or rules are broken, there need to be consequences (e.g. time-out, grounding, loss of privileges, etc.). But the admonishment should be for the failure to complete the task and not be designed to 'shame' or 'guilt' the young person into compliance. You should be seen as a partner who is helping a youngster to respect rules and authority. As a parent you are teaching them truthfulness and honesty as concepts to be cherished in their own right and not out of fear.

For the older child

As children age, these general principles remain accurate, but a new dimension needs to be taken into account. A teenager's ability to reason has begun to mature to a level that is comparable to that of an adult, although they are not fully there. So when a teenager is untruthful, there are different areas that must be considered in understanding and altering the behaviour.

Cost–benefit analyses

First of all there is the matter of what has been termed a 'cost–benefit analysis'. Briefly stated, this is where the adolescent weighs what they will 'lose' by telling the truth against what they may 'gain' by lying.

Let's say that you have told your teenage son to do three things:

- Take out the rubbish.
- Clean up his room.
- Tidy the garden.

After a hard day at work you come home to find that none of these tasks has been completed. The first thing out of most parents' mouths is usually something like 'Did you do the jobs that I told you to do today?'

There are two possible responses to this by the teen:

- He can tell the truth, say that he did not do the jobs and receive a penalty.

- He can lie, say that he did do them and hope to get the tasks done later.

The latter is especially probable if he has done some part of the tasks. If he tells the truth he is guaranteed to either receive a consequence or at least start an argument.

If he lies there are again two possible outcomes:

- You will believe him, he will not get punished and he may be able to get the chores done before you know what has occurred.

- You will not believe him and he will suffer your displeasure.

The choices suggest that your child has to choose between a 100 per cent guarantee of something negative happening and a 50 per cent chance of getting away without any consequences. As an adult you would hopefully choose honesty and admit you had not completed the jobs. However, adolescent reasoning may result in the opposite choice.

THINK ABOUT IT

In the village where I live there are stringently enforced parking regulations with a relatively small fine attached for staying too long in the allotted spaces. At Christmas, when people are rushing from store to store and queues are long, and you realize that you are about to exceed the parking limit, you then face a dilemma:

- Do you leave the line, rush out and pay for a new ticket?

- Do you stay in the line and risk receiving a fine?

Some people choose to stay, complete their Christmas purchases and pay the minimal fine if their car is checked. Others are deterred by the thought of a fine, put their potential purchases back and rush out to buy a new pay-and-display ticket. The point is that a cost–benefit analysis has once again prevailed, this time in the world of adult living.

This translates quite easily to many situations in which adolescents find themselves. Do not therefore be surprised that sometimes the choice is to disobey rules or instructions, or even to be untruthful, for they have decided that the potential rewards are worth the risk of the consequences they will receive.

So when you arrive home and find that the tasks have not been done, instead of asking a question to which you already know the answer, it is better to make a statement of fact. For example, you might say, 'I told you to empty the bin, clean up your room and tidy the garden. You did not do this so now I want you to do some other things (e.g. wash four windows, clean the bath and iron all his shirts). However, if you apologize, tell me what you should have done and then go and do it, you will only have to wash three windows.'

In this scenario you have now changed the odds to promote the truth. Your teenager will again have two choices: lie and receive 100 per cent of the further impositions or tell the truth, apologize and receive a lesser penalty. Using adolescent logic *against* a teenager almost always results in the truth.

Keep in mind that negative consequences do not mean you will necessarily keep the disobedient behaviour from happening again. Instead you will be teaching your child a lesson in living that is very worthwhile.

Legalistic reasoning

The teenager also often engages in an unusual type of reasoning often termed 'legalistic'. With this the child feels that since he meant to do the chores and intends to do them later, and since you did not specify *exactly* by what time that he had to do the jobs but simply said 'today', he is not really lying at all. He may still do them later today and thus meet your directives. In this case, not telling you the exact truth and thereby avoiding an unjust punishment (unjust because he would have completed the jobs later) would be perfectly acceptable. This convoluted way of thinking is very frustrating to the average parent but quite reasonable to the typical teenager.

One way to cope with this maddening type of reasoning is to first of all specify clearly the time by which you want things done. Therefore an even better version of the statement suggested earlier would be 'I told you to empty the bin *by noon*, clean up your room *by two* and tidy the garden *before four*.' It is also necessary to state contingencies in case one or more of the activities cannot be done (e.g. he had no bin bags for the rubbish and he was supposed to do this first so he didn't do any of the other things you asked him to do).

Affairs of the heart

The methods described above – the 'response method' of making statements to the adolescent instead of asking questions, and structuring consequences – work with most typical teenage 'truth-or-lie' problems but there are some where they do not. These are the lies that surround what are perhaps best called 'affairs of the heart'.

Teenagers often feel love and hate, and experience loyalty, etc., with an intensity that mystifies parents. To the adolescent, the love that they have for their girlfriend or boyfriend is something unique to the world and nobody else has ever experienced anything like this before. This is not just romantic nonsense but a result of the fact that *they* have never experienced these emotions before and believe sincerely that they are the first humans ever to have felt this way.

Therefore a lie that is told to protect their love or to be loyal to a gang, or even for revenge on a detested enemy, is justified by the outcome. In their minds it is not necessarily untruthful for it serves a higher purpose. Many teenagers will not accept parental annoyance when they cover up about seeing a girlfriend or boyfriend instead of completing schoolwork. After all, how can parents possibly appreciate the demands of true love?

When confronted by 'affairs of the heart' situations as a parent, it is necessary to give a consequence for the untruthfulness (grounding, restrictions, jobs, etc.) as well as an explanation of how the teenager's reply affected you and your trust. Although your teenager will not truly grasp what you are saying at the time, eventually they will as they mature.

USEFUL TIP One word of caution: you risk seriously affecting your son or daughter's developing self-esteem if you confront untruthfulness or a lack of openness with too strong a personal criticism. Instead you should be consistent and empathetic using statements that let your son or daughter know that they are basically good but with a bad habit. You should let them know that even though they have exercised poor judgement, they will have opportunities to make different choices that allow them to break this habit. With this approach, the result in terms of the adult they become will justify the frustrations you suffer.

The techniques outlined above are effective for dealing with the majority of dishonesty patterns exhibited by typical children and adolescents. With emotionally disturbed children, the motives for a child's responses can be much more difficult to decipher and the parental responses often have to be tailored to the individual. Examples include the child who has an addiction to alcohol or pornography, or the child who has suffered a traumatic event that they are ashamed to reveal to their parent. In these situations, seeking the assistance of a counsellor is strongly encouraged, for the cost–benefit analysis that is usually done does not apply and the lies serve a self-protection function not easily resolved by parents alone.

6. Where Have All the Good Things Gone?

All stealing is comparative. If you come to absolutes,
pray who does not steal?

—Ralph Waldo Emerson

'We can't leave anything out. She will nick everything from money to pencils and pens! You have to watch her every minute, for as soon as you turn your back it's gone!'

Parents of children from three to adulthood have related this complaint and find the sticky-fingered habits of their children to be exquisitely frustrating. In response to the thefts, parents usually try – typically without much success – such things as:

- Smacking.
- Shaming activities.
- Withdrawal of privileges.

Sometimes parents have resorted to taking their child to the local court to demonstrate what becomes of thieves, or had police constables drop by to lecture their child. These actions also result in failure and continued frustration to the parent who is desperate to raise an 'honest child'.

Parents are concerned about the origins of this

behaviour for they see themselves as honest people who encourage these same values in their children. They cannot understand why their values have apparently been ignored by their offspring and readily blame outside influences such as peers, videogames or television for their child's abhorrent actions. Such influences can indeed lead to a child who steals, although this is usually not the instigator of the problem. Instead it tends to be the communication between the parent and child that is most often at fault. If you are willing to accept that your interactions may be part of the problem then there is real hope for changing your child into the person you always wanted.

The parents of a child who takes things should first clarify what are their expectations. In the parent's mind this is usually clear: they want honesty and a lack of stealing. However, an objective examination of the youngster's viewpoint suggests that he or she has a much murkier understanding of even simple situations.

Suppose that a parent wants their child to do a project which needs to be done in pen, and the child says that he doesn't have one. The parent may say something like 'Just look in my room where I keep my wallet' or 'Get one out of my purse.' Rarely does the parent think about the implications of what they have just said, for they are focused on getting the task done efficiently. The parent is just glad that the obstacle has been overcome. However, they have unknowingly given permission to a child to go into areas which were once forbidden.

The parent will typically give reinforcement by a comment such as 'Good show. Now let's get on with it.' In the parent's mind, they have allowed a one-off exception to a general rule (i.e. 'Thou Shalt Not Go into Thy Mother's Purse'). However, in the child's mind the rule has been voided and no longer applies.

There is a concept known to psychologists as 'generalization'. This concept was clearly demonstrated by a behaviourist known as John B. Watson (1878–1958) with graduate student Rosalie Rayner in a 1920 experiment with a nine-month-old child called 'Little Albert'. In the experiment the child was exposed to a white rat, rabbit, and other white objects without any fear being displayed. However, when the rat was shown later, a loud noise was made, causing the infant to cry out of fear. When the other white objects were subsequently shown to the child, he cried even though no loud noise had been associated with them.

This notion also applies to positive actions. Once you have learned a response to one situation, and are then confronted by a similar problem, you tend to apply the same action to solve it. As an example, let us assume that the child needs some money to pay for an item needed for school.

When confronted by the need for a pen for a school task, you told your child where to go and then praised them for solving the problem. It is not much of a leap for the child to go into mum's purse or dad's wallet to get the money to pay for the item, since they are again solving a problem related to school. Most of the time the parents would have given them the money if asked and often the amount is very small and is not missed by the parent.

REMEMBER THIS!!! When the child has solved the problem and been rewarded by getting the desired item, and no negative feedback has come from the parents, the probability that the behaviour will be repeated goes up dramatically the next time they need or want something. Parents are by nature usually reluctant to believe that their child has 'stolen' from them and will most likely assume that the missing money was an error on their part rather than make a fuss and confront their child.

Generalization as regards stealing occurs very rapidly when a situation such as this has occurred. The step from pinching money for a school item to something the child wants to buy from the shop is a relatively small one, as is taking money from another place in the house where money is kept, instead of the parent's purse or wallet. Gradually things besides money, such as earrings, keys, rings and other personal items, begin to be taken.

Eventually parents develop a suspicion that their youngster is stealing from them and will search their room for evidence to confirm this. When the 'stolen' items are found, the parent is almost always furious and will confront the youngster with a question such as 'Did you steal my ring?'

In the child's mind they did not 'steal' but instead simply borrowed or used something that their parent possessed. Thus they can truthfully say that they did not steal it. This only serves to further infuriate the parent.

The next event is typically a lecture and a punishment for the stealing. The child most often feels that this is unjust and undeserved and thus the parental response fails to deter the behaviour from happening again.

Compounding this scenario is that many parents tend to equivocate in their responses and try to make a distinction between things of little value that are okay to take and things that are clearly inappropriate. Unfortunately, the concept of differential values is a very difficult one to comprehend and only makes sense when they become an older adolescent. An example from clinical practice may clarify this point.

 One child referred for counselling had been taking small amounts of money from his parents for snacks, things from a shop and for use at school. Over time he progressed to a point where he took several thousand pounds that he found in an envelope in his father's desk. As work with him progressed, it became apparent that at age ten he really did not comprehend the distinction between taking a few coins and taking several thousand pounds. In his mind it was just money and the relative values were unimportant. The theft was discovered only when he gave several hundred pounds to children at school in an attempt to win favour and friendships.

Parents often respond to continued thefts with ever harsher punishments and then turn to measures aimed at removing temptation such as:

- Locking doors.
- Hiding wallets and purses.
- Placing their children under a state of constant observation.

Some parents have gone to the extremes of putting alarms on doors so that the child cannot leave his room without them knowing. Unfortunately by this time the pattern of behaviour has not only become well established but the actions of the parents are perceived as a sort of perverse game in which the child's role is to try to overcome the parental barriers and obstacles. Thus children can become adept at devising ways of breaking into their parents' locked bedroom or at finding supposedly secret hiding places.

What, then, should a parent do if the punishment is ineffective and the stealing seems to constantly be getting worse? The answer goes back to the original, basic desire of the parents that the child should grow up to be an honest person. The responsibility of the parent is to focus on *teaching honesty* and not punishing stealing. The two are definitely not the same and the right parental reaction can be crucial.

Let us take the most common theft that occurs in a

home, which is money. Instead of hiding money away, the parents could leave the money out in the open, such as on a table, and then make their child responsible for the money staying there. They could say something like, 'It is your responsibility to make sure that this money stays here. Let's count it together. If any of it is gone, no matter how much or who takes it, you will have to do the following jobs.'

The parent can then specify a reasonable consequence that involves doing something *positive* for the household, such as cleaning the toilet or bath, washing windows, etc. This activity does not involve smacking or taking something away from the child but instead emphasizes the idea of doing something that benefits the family. In this situation you are teaching and reinforcing the concept of *responsibility* instead of trying to stamp out stealing by punishment.

It is necessary to be specific and to let your child know that regardless of what happens to the money, even if someone else should take it or it is accidentally lost, they are the one who is accountable for it. This then teaches the idea that someone is ultimately responsible for everything.

Parents typically find that the money usually stays where they have placed it. If however the money is gone, then after just a few times of doing the resulting housework, usually the child learns to leave it alone. He or she then begins to feel pride for having been trusted with the responsibility for the money.

Parents can then instigate a beneficial form of generalization by making the child responsible for the mother's purse and the father's wallet when these are left out. The parents can then assign more and more items to the care and monitoring of the child until the thieving eventually disappears. This is a very powerful technique that empowers both parents and children.

In the case of theft that has started later in life, such as in adolescence, analysing the motives behind the behaviour is even more critical than for younger children. As mentioned in the previous chapter, adolescents are capable of a reasoning that is similar to that of adults, but their thinking often reflects different priorities, which can be understood by recourse to the concept of a 'hierarchy of needs'.

 Abraham Maslow is a humanist psychologist who in 1943 wrote a paper setting out what he felt to be our fundamental human needs. He initially specified five but later expanded upon this (see opposite).

Maslow contended that people concentrate upon satisfying the lower or more basic needs before moving on to the next level in the hierarchy. Subsequent research has indicated that people do not need to completely satisfy a more basic need before being motivated by a higher one if the lower is addressed to some extent.

In our society the physiological and safety needs of the majority of people are generally addressed. Therefore it is the higher-level needs of belonging and love, esteem

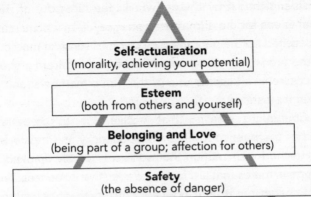

Maslow's hierarchy of needs

and self-actualization that usually need to be examined in understanding the behaviour of adolescents.

Consider the action of pilfering, which is common among teenagers and causes parents endless worry and anger. Understanding why the behaviour has occurred is the key to responding to this type of theft. Was the stealing done alone or with a group of mates? Peer pressure is a very powerful force. This is especially true when the behaviour has been reframed by the group as a harmless joke.

The desire to belong and be accepted can often cause an adolescent to perform acts that they would rarely consider doing if by themselves. In the hierarchy of personal needs for the adolescent, acceptance by others must be satisfied before pleasing their parents' sense of morality. To the teenager, the act of taking something from a shop is necessary to become one of the group members, and is therefore justified.

Countering stealing that occurs due to the influence of the peer group is somewhat tricky and has to be approached with caution. Many parents simply demand a change in mates that are felt to be negative influences. The child's behaviour is seen as an abnormality that has resulted from particular associations. Unfortunately this ignores the 'belonging' need of the adolescent. Prohibiting associations can perversely result in the teenager bonding more closely with the 'undesirable' group.

The vast majority of people, including adolescents, do not like to feel secluded from others. Thus when a parent demands a change of social circle, teenagers feel isolated and alone. This is combined with the developmental task of adolescence whereby the child separates from their parents and creates their individual identity. The result is often a conclusion that their friends' values should be followed and not those of their parents.

Rather than just banning association with particular peers, parents should give considerable thought to those groups that hold and express values closest to their own. Perhaps these are Boy or Girl Scouts, church youth associations, charitable organizations, activist groups, sports teams, military associations, etc. Simultaneously with the reduction of contact with the negative peer influences, the parents need to involve their child and themselves in the organizations that espouse the beliefs they cherish.

The involvement of the parents with these groups is important as part of the effort to demonstrate that they really believe in the values represented by the groups. Role-modelling is an important learning tool for all of us. Parents simply cannot tell their child to go to an acceptable group and feel that this will solve the problem of reinforcing their own core values of honesty and respect for others. They must 'walk the walk' as well as 'talk the talk'.

The values of honour, honesty, respect and so on should be discussed with the adolescent in the myriad situations that come up on a day-to-day basis – you cannot have just one talk with your child and then believe you are done. If these actions are taken there is a strong probability that the adolescent will gradually change their values to those of the new peer group and stealing may become a thing of the past. The 'discussions', however, must not be just lectures or admonitions, but a genuine and open exploration of core values. Areas to be explored include:

- Why people should not steal.
- The concept of ownership.
- Pride in your morality.
- Self-esteem.

Stealing in isolation

Suppose that the stealing has occurred in isolation or without the evident influence of others. If this is the situation then the origins of the behaviour must again be looked for in the individual's 'personal needs hierarchy', which is often different from that of the parent.

Perhaps the theft was done out of a perceived necessity. The word 'perceived' is used judiciously, for what a parent believes is important or crucial is often not the same belief as that held by the adolescent. A teenager may truly believe that having the latest videogame or operating system is absolutely at the top of their importance list while to a parent it is irrelevant or trivial.

 It is critical when talking with your teenager to get inside their head and to understand why they felt that having the item was such a necessity. Then the question of why the child felt the need to take the item instead of coming to the parent to find a way to obtain it can be thoroughly explored over the course of several conversations.

Many forces in the child's life contradict the beliefs of the average parent. For example, look at the values often portrayed in videogames. Stealing (or commonly referred to as acquiring, accumulating, gathering, pillaging, robbing and raiding) items in videogames is often portrayed as noble, exciting and just. Cinema and music are two other major influences that can often convey these same messages.

The jump from the cyber world or that of the Arts to the real world is not that far for an adolescent. Parents may believe that their child has acquired values of honesty when in reality, by not drawing a clear distinction between what is fantasy and what is reality, they have passively reinforced an acceptance of thievery.

 Parents should take advantage of daily opportunities that arise while watching reality TV shows, for example, or playing videogames. Making comments which clarify the distinction between what is acceptable in a game and your core values such as honesty can create significant changes in a child. As a parent you should remember that quite probably you either bought the videogame for them or at least gave them permission to buy it. Thus in the child's mind you have implicitly endorsed the values portrayed. If these values are not consistent with your beliefs then you must make this very clear in your conversations as well as justify why you allowed the game/music/movie into your household.

Another common origin of theft with an individualistic origin would be where the teenager is in love. In this situation the taking of something is justified if the end result is a closer bonding with the loved one. Taking money from parents to give to your loved one and taking things such as jewellery that the adolescent does not have the money to buy can all be justified by the need to express dedication and affection to a girlfriend or boyfriend. Punishment to the teenager in this situation again seems unjust, for to them the love that they feel is unique in the world.

In correcting and changing this type of behaviour it is necessary to tread carefully. If you try to force the child to confess his 'crime' to his loved one and return the stolen item he will feel trapped between a potential loss of love and compliance with his parents. He may feel that running away or even suicide may be the only solution to his problems. As you talk to your child you should acknowledge the reality of his love but discuss with him the effect that finding out the item was stolen would have upon the love object. Discuss alternatives to the stealing and state the need to return the stolen item.

USEFUL TIP Suggest specific solutions such as getting a part-time job, saving money and then buying something to replace the gift to the loved one. At the same time, you could help your child to write a note or practise a speech to explain how out of love they made a wrong decision to give something that was not theirs to give. If the parents approach the stealing in this manner the teenager will usually react with an acknowledgement that the stealing was incorrect. Rarely does yelling, cursing or labelling the adolescent a thief accomplish the same result.

There are many other reasons for adolescents to steal things besides the influence of peers or media, or out of a perceived necessity. These motives can encompass such things as:

- Revenge.
- Jealousy.
- Hatred.
- Depression.

Once again, simply punishing the behaviour by groundings, lectures, restrictions or physical punishments is most often ineffective. Permanent changes in attitude do not occur if the parent does not put in the time and effort needed to understand the world view of the adolescent.

An example would be where your teenager is feeling depressed due to weight issues. Stealing items may be a way of temporarily making him or her feel good by the acquisition of things to replace a lack of status. Finding ways to help the adolescent feel better while pointing out the false sense of temporary improvement that larceny pro-vides will lead to the more permanent outcome of a person who is honest.

The key factor in approaching all of these situations is to first understand the reasoning and feelings of your child before intervening. If you address the issues that underlie their actions you are quite likely to then be viewed as a champion for your child rather than someone who is simply part of the problem.

This does not mean that you should accept the stealing, approve of it or allow your child to keep the stolen item. Instead, if you are viewed as being on his or her side while not compromising your own values of honesty and integrity then it is much more likely that the adolescent will accept your suggestions for alternative ways of acting. Groundings and restrictions are much more acceptable to teenagers when they are imposed by a parent who is felt to be compassionate and understanding.

After identifying the underlying motives for the stealing and suggesting alternative actions, parents should then ask the youth what would be an appropriate penalty for their actions. Parents who do this are almost always surprised at the harshness of the consequence suggested by the adolescent. For example, the teenager may state that they should be restricted to the house for six months or never be allowed to go to a particular place again.

Parents then find that when they impose a much more modest consequence that their child is not only grateful but much more receptive to trying the parents' suggestions for change. As a parental figure you have become a partner in their struggles to mature, rather than an arbitrary or antiquated figure of authority who is out of touch with the realities of being young.

7. Why is the Trash Bin Always Empty?

We are only just beginning to understand the power of love because we are just beginning to understand the weakness of force and aggression.

—B.F. Skinner, *Walden Two*

When you were a child, did your room look like a disaster area with clothes on the floor, toys all over the place and with the barely identifiable remains of food and their accompanying utensils lying about? Perhaps you were one of the rare 'neat freaks' whose room was spotless but you never seemed able to turn your homework in on time. Perchance you were the sort of youngster who began studying for a test just a few hours before it was to take place, or the sort who could never seem to remember what chore it was that you were supposed to do.

Then again maybe you never had any of these problems but your child does and you cannot begin to fathom how it is possible that a child of yours could be so opposite in his values from those that you hold dear. In all of these cases, the desire of the parent is almost always the same: to have their child grow up to be an orderly, clean, responsible adult. Parents worry constantly that poor habits will persist into adulthood and result in failure at work, home and life in general. They fear that others will hold them responsible for the failings of their offspring and will criticize them for poor parenting.

The reaction of parents to children who appear to be lazy or irresponsible is almost always the same. Parents sit down and try, at least initially, to calmly and rationally explain the eventual consequences of the untidy habits. They explain that 'cleanliness is next to Godliness' or that 'we just don't live that way' and that the child will never be able to marry, get into university or hold down a decent job if they don't change their ways.

Most times their child will agree with them and seem to understand but rarely does anything change. The parent then usually becomes frustrated that their quite sensible explanations are apparently ignored by their offspring and start feeling as though the child is deliberately being messy and irresponsible in defiance of their wishes. The situation has now become a contest of wills that they cannot afford to lose.

Quite often, parents are at odds with one another on how to approach their child at this point and the yelling of the one parent is criticized by the other, with statements such as 'You are just making it worse' or 'I was that way when I was a child and I turned out okay' being bandied about. The criticized parent, whose yelling was after all only meant to encourage their child to be more responsible, often feels hurt and misunderstood. They will then often take out their anger on their partner or the youngster. The arguments and fighting tend to escalate to the point that everyone in the household is uncomfortable.

When the lecture or yelling approaches fail, most parents attempt to use a combination of threats and rewards to motivate: for example groundings or the withdrawal of privileges on the one hand, and the promise of treats on the other. Quite often there is a short-term improvement in the child's behaviour in response to these actions but rarely does he or she seem to fundamentally adopt the parent's priorities and permanently change his or her ways. What then can a parent do?

The principles of behaviour modification in which good behaviours are rewarded and negative behaviours are extinguished can often seem ineffective when it comes to changing the habits of children. However, their failure usually stems from the manner in which the principles are applied rather than any underlying problem with the principles themselves.

Consider the common situation of the messy room with a younger child. Parents are clear in what they want, in that they wish to build a lifelong habit of cleanliness and orderliness. They will patiently explain this but when the child does not then tidy the room, they may threaten to take away a possession or give a smacking if it is not done in the next ten minutes. Tears of frustration often result, with most parents immediately questioning themselves as to whether they have been too harsh or have demanded something beyond the developmental capability of the child. Consoling hugs may follow, combined with statements such as an explanation that the parent is doing this 'for your own good' and a reassurance that 'someday you will understand what I mean'.

Many times the child will do part of the task requested, with the result that the parent will explain that not everything has been done and that cleaning your room means picking up *all* things from the floor and not just the clothes. Typically after this an extension of the time for doing the task is granted.

The parent enforcing the activity rationalizes the extension by wishing to appear reasonable and show compassion. If the task is then completed appropriately, they feel that the extension was appropriate and justified by the results. If the task still has not been completed when the new time limit is up, the parent most often becomes angry at two things:

- The task not having been done.

- Their generosity having been taken advantage of.

Punishment is usually swiftly forthcoming and in excess of what was originally envisioned due to the perceived extra offence. After this scenario is completed the parent will believe that they have successfully taught a lesson – until the next time the room is a disaster area and the whole interaction repeats itself.

One of the great insights of B.F. Skinner when he developed the concept of operant conditioning from his research with animals and then extended it to humans is that when behaviour is rewarded or reinforced, children tend to repeat the action willingly due to a perception that they are doing what they *want* to do. Punishment will result in the youth temporarily behaving appropriately but the child will believe that their freedom is being suppressed and they are being 'good' only out of fear.

The failure by parents to teach a lesson in how to be clean and orderly (or get assignments done on time, or any of a thousand other things we envision our children learning in order to become responsible adults) is not due to the punishments or rewards doled out, nor to the underlying principles involved, but is instead due to issues of timing, sequencing and the underlying motivators in your child.

Let us look at this scenario from the child's point of view. Cleaning up their room is an onerous task with no perceived benefit. After all won't the room just get messy again? So then why should they clean it in the first place?

The untidiness is normal, acceptable and does not bother them. Any effort expended in cleaning the room just detracts from their time playing and having fun. There is not a natural incentive to clean the room in the sense of their receiving a satisfied feeling from having a neat and clean abode as might happen with an adult.

If the parent tells them that there will be a reward for doing it then often they will balance the proposed reward against the effort needed to accomplish the undertaking and may decide that it is not worth it. In essence, your child will be saying 'No thanks' to a perceived deal. When consequences are then threatened they will feel that they are being unjustly vilified. Didn't they just tell you that they were happy to forego the treat in exchange for not cleaning the room? Therefore what is your problem?

There is a way to counter these difficulties using rewards or the withdrawal of privileges that will work in changing poor habits. However, this requires that the adult view events from the child's perspective.

Consider the example of a child whose life centres around the three things that he enjoys the most:

- Using social networking sites on the internet.

- Playing videogames.

- Chatting with friends on the phone.

If the parent finds that their child's room is a wreck, chores are not being done and class projects are not being completed due to all the time consumed by these activities then the parent needs to analyse how their child feels about these things. The parent must clearly state to the child that these activities are *privileges* and not a birthright.

Their child is told that the three identified activities are treats that must be earned and that each day there is zero time allocated for him to do them. In order to earn time for each activity, tasks must be done to the parent's satisfaction. When completed, he earns a set amount of time that he can use for any one of the activities. Thus tidying the room might earn 45 minutes on one of the three things, while completing a homework assignment might earn an additional 30 minutes. The rules are that the time cannot be carried over to the next day but must be used on the day earned.

To make the arrangement fair and not a punishment, the parent can stress that all family time is free. Thus the child has the freedom to play a board game, watch a programme on TV with the rest of the family or simply read a book in a communal area. There are many things that a child can do to fill up their time at night and after school is out.

To the child you have made a proposal that reflects the way life is for adults:

- How many people are compensated before they complete their work?

- Is it not typical for your company to reimburse you at the end of a pay period for work done rather than the other way around?

- If you go to the cinema or to a football match do you get to watch the activity first and then pay as you leave?

The answer to these questions is 'of course not'. Therefore having someone earn time to do the activities that they wish simply follows real-life scripts.

To the child you have become someone who is dispensing favours or giving out rewards rather than always threatening punishments or nagging about doing undesirable tasks. In adopting this approach, eventually you will be thought of not as taking things away but as granting access to desired activities by virtue of a reasonable arrangement. Almost all children readily come to this conclusion and the change in their personal habits can be quite dramatic.

The attitude of the parent needs to be such that they are perceived as sympathetic to the child's wishes with regard to their favoured activities but firm on the principle that rules must be obeyed – even though the parent is the one who created the rules. They must be fair but firm in their dispensing of the time earned for the fun activities. It is necessary that both parents be in agreement with the rules, for if one tries to implement these actions and the other grants the privilege just because he or she feels like it then the corrective actions will not work.

Changing the sequencing of rewards is very powerful and can result in rapid changes in the actions of both young children and adolescents. The major difference with teenagers is that you should involve them actively in negotiating the activities to be earned and the requirements of the task to be accomplished. Doing this prepares the adolescent for an adulthood of responsibility where they will reward themselves with pleasurable activities such as a trip to the pub *after* work is done rather than before.

When a parent asks an adolescent what they feel they should do to earn a privilege, they are often pleasantly surprised at the response they receive. Teenagers can be very mature in their reasoning concerning cause and effect. It is your responsibility to nurture this way of thinking by encouraging bargaining skills. You must try to remember that what you are developing is a new adult whom you are preparing to handle real-life circumstances independently. Doing this creates pride not only in the child but also in the parent for a job well done.

8. The Daily Horror Show

Psychologists often separate the fears and anxieties of children into two categories: those that are realistic and those that are unrealistic. All people are born with certain *realistic* innate fears such as falling or loud noises. These fears perform a survival function when we are infants and are felt to be normal due to inherent dangers in the environment. *Unrealistic* fears or concerns are those that interfere with everyday functioning despite the actual threat of harm being small and the typical person judging them to be of little or no concern.

Take for example the situation of a mouse. Some people are terrified of wild rodents and certainly there is ample historical evidence that they can cause widespread death through the transmission of bacteria and viruses. Being concerned about the presence of mice in one's house is something that the average person would find quite understandable and acceptable. Indeed we would find the person who fails to be distressed at finding mice in their abode to be unusual at best. Consider however the following situation where the fear was clearly excessive.

The young boy who came into the centre was screaming hysterically 'Get the mouse out! Get the mouse out!' He was about five years old and his eyes ceaselessly roamed everywhere, presumably looking for mice. Any attempts to touch him were met with blood-curdling shrieks and he constantly hopped from one foot to the other. The tale told by the social worker who accompanied him was tragic and yet all too illustrative of the power of adult role-modelling.

It appears that the single mother of this boy had a deathly fear of mice. One day while she and the child were in the kitchen, a mouse ran across the floor. The mother proceeded to jump on to a stool and scream 'Get it out! Get the mouse out!' at the top of her voice. Most probably the boy never saw the rodent and even if he did he was too young to be able to do anything about it. Apparently the screaming and crying of the mother went on for an extended time before neighbours came to investigate. The boy was found cowering in the corner of the room with his eyes wild and unseeing and he was unable to communicate what had happened.

The child welfare people were called and he was subsequently taken to the local psychiatric centre for treatment. While there, his therapy consisted primarily of reassuring him that he was safe and that the mouse was gone, and engaging him in play. The purpose of the play was to normalize the situation as much as possible and to demonstrate in this new setting, by role-modelling, that nobody was fearful or anxious about mice or any other thing. After several hours the therapy began to work and the boy was able to communicate once again.

Psychologist Albert Bandura developed a theory of human behaviour known as Social Learning Theory. Many of his insights relate to the concept of role-modelling as a way of learning. Simply stated, three of the key concepts that he explored and developed are:

1. People can learn through observation as opposed to needing direct reinforcement.

2. Mental states and activities are important to learning.

3. Observational learning can, but does not necessarily have to, lead to changes in behaviour.

The influence of an adult on a young person is substantial and can exaggerate or extinguish their concerns. The situation of the mother's over-reaction to the mouse illustrates how she role-modelled a horror that the child internalized rapidly and completely.

The therapists used role-modelling activities to counter the fear inadvertently instilled by the mother and were successful to an extent. However, to completely eliminate the terror required the cooperation of the mother after she had learned to overcome her own irrational fears. Eventually there was a return to the kitchen, where the therapist helped the mother and son together to experience a calm setting without anxiety. This was not done in a single step but instead involved a technique called 'systematic desensitization'.

The following discussion of desensitization techniques is intended primarily to help parents understand what the therapeutic treatment of anxiety might entail, rather than providing a 'how to' guide. A parent who is properly trained in these techniques can practise them with their child at home. However, it is not recommended that the untrained parent assume that they can do this on their own without professional guidance.

The first order of business in desensitization is to make sure that the child is not re-traumatized continually. This means that parents or other role models (e.g. teachers) must stop implanting the idea that the child cannot protect

86

him or herself and needs the help of outside rescuers to survive.

As an illustration, let us take the example of the child who is afraid of monsters in his room. Many parents try to rationalize and may tell him that 'mummy and daddy are here to protect you' and that they will never let any monsters get to him. Inadvertently, by their words the parents have confirmed the reality of monsters. They have conveyed to him the idea that he *does* need to be protected when all they were trying to do was to give him reassurance. If there are no monsters then why would a parent say that they would not let them harm their child? Such is the reasoning of a pre-teen. Instead of saying that you will protect him, the better approach is to tell the child that you will teach him how to cope with his fears.

Doing this involves a series of steps, introducing fairly innocuous items to begin with and gradually moving closer to the ultimate, most feared event or situation. Quite often in a therapy setting this series of steps is done through imagination and visual imagery due to the difficulty or impossibility of duplicating the concerning setting. However, if the concerning event or anxiety-provoking situation is something that can be seen or touched (e.g. a mouse), often the approach must be modified to bring the real item into the session. To do this systematically you might start with a stuffed toy mouse and then move to a more realistic rubber or plastic one. After this you might introduce a caged mouse at the far end of the room and then gradually move it closer to the child. With the presentation of each object you need to help the child to find something that brings laughter or fun to his mind (e.g. recalling a funny event on holiday or at a party) and then to recall and experience these feelings in the presence of the feared object.

The key is to make sure that the pleasure of the image or activity outweighs the amount of dread in the object. If this is done, then by the association of the two the young person will gradually lose their apprehension and the desensitization process occurs.

With older children or teenagers you may use the idea of identification with a positive role model such as a film star or football player to assist in overcoming fears. The youth is taught to imagine how that person would react to a dreaded situation such as giving a presentation before the class. In the child's imagination, he sees himself as the actor or athlete confronting a series of situations that systematically works up to the most panic-inducing event.

An alternative approach often used by therapists is to teach the technique of progressive muscle relaxation, in which all the muscles of the body are relaxed to produce a state of comfort and tranquillity. In this treatment, children and adults learn to recognize when there is tension in their bodies by the process of tensing muscle groups and then relaxing them. They are then given a key word or phrase to initiate recall of this relaxed state and practise this until it is readily obtainable. This is next paired with the feared succession of events and the pairing diminishes the anxiety over repeated presentations.

These techniques are not exhaustive but are examples of things that a parent can expect out of psychotherapy with their children and will hopefully help to de-mystify the actions of therapists. As mentioned previously, such techniques are best implemented by trained professionals rather than well-meaning but untrained parents. There are however a number of other activities that the parent can do independently with the anxious child.

If a parent accepts the power of the adult role model then one of the most important of all therapeutic interventions is immediately available. If you overcome your own fear of spiders, snakes, monsters, mice, clowns, etc. and then demonstrate that you have confronted your terror, there is a high probability that your child will follow in your footsteps. Being afraid is not the problem. Instead it is the acceptance of the apprehension as an unchangeable state that is the difficulty. You need to show how to recognize a problem, determine what effect it is having upon your life, decide why you need to change it and then come up with a plan for overcoming the fear.

Too often parents simply state that they are afraid and when their child overhears this it is as though it is something written in stone. By implementing changes in your own life, with or without the assistance of a therapist, you demonstrate that people can successfully challenge and overcome fears.

Consider the dread that you may have of spiders. If you have decided that this concern has become so intrusive that you need to overcome it, you must first confront the fear for what it is: something that is unrealistic. To do this you need knowledge, and that means research. You accumulate as much data as you can about their positive and negative roles in the ecosystem and find out which ones you need to realistically avoid versus those that are totally harmless. Eventually you should be able to confidently identify those that are truly dangerous versus those that are merely ferocious in appearance.

Once you are able to confront pictures of spiders in books or on a computer screen without concern, you can then move on to looking at videos of spiders while controlling your reactions by, for example, engaging in deep rhythmic breathing. You could then progress to doing such things as viewing live spiders while accompanied by a trusted individual who has no fear of them.

When you find yourself able to watch somebody in real life handling a spider then you can move on to the step of holding one yourself. The final step is to be able to confront the spiders that are found occasionally in even the cleanest of homes and to react appropriately without panic.

The essence of this activity is to demonstrate that concerns are not immutable but can be changed with thinking, planning and action. This lesson is something that a child can readily learn and apply to many of life's activities far outside the realm of fears.

9. Down in the Dumps

You cannot prevent the birds of sorrow from flying over your head, but you can prevent them from building nests in your hair.

—Chinese proverb

Recognizing depression in the pre-adolescent is a very difficult task, since they are not as articulate as adults in expressing how they feel. Instead of being able to say that they are miserable, the pre-teen will most often display their feelings in behavioural reactions. Sometimes they will give the parent descriptions that suggest a physical problem or something that is less severe than depression.

Parents are advised to question why their child might be doing any of the following:

- Losing or gaining weight suddenly.

- Having so many nightmares.

- Becoming less enthused in their play and interactions with others.

The quiet or withdrawn youth who is not aggravating others can easily be overlooked. This is especially true when parents are trying to cope with their own emotional responses to an event that has affected the family.

When queried, the youth may say they are sad, bored

or just do not feel well. Parents quite naturally assume that such statements reflect a temporary situation rather than being indicators of the more serious state of depression and will often respond with suggestions that are inappropriate. Many parents will talk about all the things their child has to play with or perhaps suggest they just go and lie down for a while. How can a parent learn to 'read between the lines' to understand just what it is that the child really means?

The first step is for parents to recognize that children can be as upset or disturbed by a situation as an adult. Events that would cause most adults to feel a sense of helplessness or hopelessness (e.g. the death of somebody we are close to, the divorce of parents, loss of a home, moving away from friends) can cause a depressed state to develop in a youngster. It is easy to assume that supposed childhood innocence will protect them from the worries that overwhelm us as adults. This is rarely true and most often the young child will feel the problem deeply but just display it differently.

While the child may become listless, feel hopeless and show the tears of sadness as readily as any adult, it is equally likely that they will become anxious, agitated and act out their fears in aggressive or destructive manners. The term 'agitated depression' is not an oxymoron; it is often used to describe individuals who react to a depressive event in a restless, reckless or even panicky manner. They may be as worried as their parents over a situation but seem to display behaviour in a manner opposite to that which we usually associate with depression.

Additionally, if the whole family has been affected then the child may have to cope both with the precipitating event and the loss of emotional support from his parents. If you as a parent are feeling significant symptoms of depression then the probability is high that your youngster is also suffering.

REMEMBER THIS!!! The parent needs to be aware of the volatility of children. At one moment the child may be laughing and apparently having fun and then the next may appear with a saddened expression and tears. The juxtaposition of the laughing and the crying is often puzzling to adults. Just because a child's moods are quixotic or labile, do not jump to the conclusion that your child is suffering from bipolar disorder. Parents must recognize that it is a normal facet of childhood to rapidly change one's emotions but that this does not negate the authenticity of the underlying emotions.

The dejection felt is real and must be addressed. There is a genuine danger that ignoring childhood depression can result in an impulsive suicide gesture or other action of self-harm.

Another reaction of children that is easy to overlook is the use of avoidance to cope with the upsetting event. Adults may turn to the abuse of alcohol to assuage their feelings of distress. Similarly it is not at all unusual to see a child turn to an almost obsessive-like involvement in something such as a videogame or overeating as a way of avoiding emotional pain.

Unfortunately when we as adults are hurting and struggling with our own ability to cope, it is very tempting to convince ourselves that our child has avoided the pain we are experiencing. We may interpret their play as normal and even encourage the activity as a way of preoccupying him while we try to sort out our own emotional concerns.

An additional reaction of the depressed young person may be to become over-dependent upon the parent. A youngster can become:

- Clingy.
- Tearful when the adult is away.
- Demanding of excessive time for no apparent reason.

He may show behavioural signs such as talking, walking or reacting slower than usual. He may have trouble sleeping or sleep too much. All of these reactions are the child's attempts to seek protection from a world which is overwhelming and too frightening to confront. The parent, or sometimes a teacher or the mother of a friend, who find themselves the sudden centre of a child's world, should question the reason behind the actions, for it may well be the child's way of coping with dejection.

How then should the parent react to a child who appears to be depressed? An examination of what is going on in the family that would frighten the child or threaten their security is a needed first step. The sources of despair in children are as varied as in adults.

Children are by their very nature incapable of making major life decisions for the family. They have no ability to influence the parent's boss to keep their father or mother employed, to solve the marital discord that is breaking up their world, or to prevent their parent from being sent off on a military deployment.

It is the parent's job to look at possible sources that might be overwhelming their son or daughter and then to sort out how they are being affected. The parent must become a detective to an extent and through gentle questioning tease out what it is that is upsetting the child's world. Once this is done, they must teach the child *how to cope* and *not* just solve the problem for them.

Too often the parent tries to remove the hurt to make their child happy again. Parents who are in the process of separating have 'for the sake of the children' decided to stay together even though there is no love left in their relationship. They have also done such things as:

- Demanded meetings with teachers to berate the school for failing to properly educate.

- Insisted that their son or daughter be on a team or included in a school play.

- Met with the parents of another child to stop perceived bullying behaviour.

Most often these activities fail to lift the child's spirits and may make the situation worse.

Once you have determined the origins of the sadness, you need to assume a teaching role in which you are helping your child through an unpleasant learning experience. This is not teaching in the sense of giving a lecture. Lectures only tend to deepen unhappiness by making the youngster feel that there is something wrong with them and how they have reacted.

Instead the teaching needs to be done with sensitivity and love. You are promoting learning to actively manage life's unpleasant events rather than just avoid them. You must use your experience and own emotional reactions to validate their feelings and then help them to understand that hurt is to be expected but can be overcome.

The essential nature of the interaction is to impart the belief that all problems can be solved, no matter how difficult they appear. This requires a delicate balancing act and must come from a parent who has his or her own feelings under at least fair control. Commiserating with your child on the unfairness of life or using your youngster as a confidant to relieve your own stress and worries is likely to be counterproductive.

In helping a depressed young person, you must walk a narrow path between unrealistic optimism and abject despair. You must validate the reality of the child's feelings while at the same time not imparting the notion that negative feelings are the only way to react. This is the essence of the hope that you are trying to instil.

The discussions that you hold need to be multiple and adaptable to the times when he or she is hurting. A flexible approach might involve:

- Spending some time together baking.

- Playing a game.

- Going for a walk or a drive together, away from the situation.

What all of these activities have in common is that they make time for the two of you to talk, and especially for you as a parent to listen.

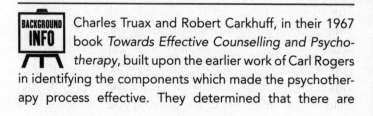

BACKGROUND INFO Charles Truax and Robert Carkhuff, in their 1967 book *Towards Effective Counselling and Psychotherapy*, built upon the earlier work of Carl Rogers in identifying the components which made the psychotherapy process effective. They determined that there are essentially four conditions that are very important in therapy, regardless of theoretical orientation: non-possessive warmth, accurate empathy, genuineness, and unconditional positive regard. These same four principles are essential in interactions with your child to counter depression.

Your attitude is perhaps more important than what you say. **Non-possessive warmth** (you love them without demanding anything in return), **unconditional positive regard** (you will love them no matter what happens), **genuineness** (you are not trying to hide anything) and **accurate empathy** (you are on the same track as your child in what you are talking about) are the ingredients of a successful parental intervention with an unhappy child. Do not feel that you have to have all the answers, for this is unrealistic. Instead you should focus on conveying the idea that, while the problem may be complex, together you can and will find an acceptable solution.

What should a parent do?

As a parent you need to focus on helping a young mind develop the skill of reasoning. Approaching the problem as one in which you are teaching logical thinking as opposed to just giving suggestions eliminates the need for the parent to be omnipotent. Throughout your own life you have faced countless problems and found solutions to all of them. If you reflect on how you did this you will usually find a surprisingly similar process occurred across almost all activities.

First you should help your child state simply and clearly the goal he or she wants to achieve. It is important that this be realistic, and this is where your parental life experiences come into play.

One example is where the source of the misery is an impending divorce. It is not unusual for the child to say they want the parents to stay together. This is unrealistic and thus your task becomes one of helping to reframe the goal while at the same time not belittling their desire.

A parent might say something along the lines of 'I know you want mummy and daddy to stay together, and for our family to be as it always has been, and it hurts to think of us as being apart. But the problems between mummy and daddy have become so bad that we are both terribly unhappy and argue all the time. We have decided it is best for us to live apart. So let's talk about what we can do to make life as good as possible for you and all of us.' The discussion should include references to the unchanging parental love, an acknowledgement of the child's fears and concerns and should avoid any dumping of parental guilt (e.g. 'You don't want mummy and daddy to be unhappy, do you?').

After the goal has been clearly stated, the next step is to delineate all of the factors affecting the situation. In the divorce example this might include such things as:

• Where the parents are going to live.

- Siblings.
- Custody.
- Visitation and transportation.
- New people coming into their lives.
- Schools.
- Friendships.
- Possessions.

As the parent guides the discussion, the relative importance of these concerns to the child can often be an eye-opener. To the parent, a stuffed toy that their child values and takes with them on visits is inconsequential but to the child it may have enormous security implications. Finding out the relative meaning of each component of the overall concern is critical.

The next step is to help find compromises to each component of the problem that are workable and acceptable. It is important that the solutions are ones the youngster creates, albeit with the coaching and guidance of the parent. When the child says that the one thing that would help reduce their fear in a parental separation is that they could take something from mum's house to dad's house when they go from one to the other, the result is much more satisfying and empowering than if the parent had originated the same suggestion.

The final step is to review periodically, and initially frequently, the situation that has caused such stress. The one constant in all lives is change and helping a young person to understand and accept this is a very valuable lesson. Previous solutions can become no longer valid due to changed circumstances and this requires altering plans accordingly. Helping your child to accept this is a primary duty of all responsible parents.

These actions are very powerful across a large number of situations leading to childhood depression. Teaching this process and practising it will not only resolve the situation causing the immediate distress but prepare the young mind to handle many other problems encountered throughout life.

This method of addressing depression is applicable to adolescents as well as the younger child, although with teenagers the amount of guidance or coaching needed to come up with a workable solution should be less.

The child who is about eleven or older tends to enter a stage where logic seems sometimes to have evaporated and irrational thinking rules the day. A parent who wants to help their depressed adolescent needs to be aware of the emotional intensity that pervades so much of a teenager's life. For example, as discussed in earlier chapters, the love they have discovered for another is intense and beyond reason. Hatred for an enemy can be all-consuming and far beyond the precipitating incident.

The volatility of emotions at this age can precipitate an emotional reaction that to a parent seems totally at odds with the importance of the originating event.

Examples of this are:

- A failure to be invited to a special party.

- A boyfriend or girlfriend who 'cheats' on them by texting somebody else.

- Not making the team.

- Questions about one's looks or virility.

The adolescent lacks the ability to adopt the parent's perspective precisely because of their inexperience. The situation to the teenager is a critical, life-changing one and must be dealt with now.

With their lack of problem-solving experience, the juvenile can rapidly feel trapped by overwhelming emotions. A possible result is that when the available options appear to have been exhausted, suicide becomes a viable and acceptable alternative. This is a danger that tragically too many parents have found to be the price to pay for ignoring their adolescent's emotions and believing they will simply grow out of it. To counter this it is necessary to keep the lines of communication open, such that your child knows that he or she can come to you to talk about their anguish with the expectation of receiving an open and caring reception.

Working with the teenager who is dejected can be a heart-wrenching experience, and requires patience. Rarely will the adolescent say 'thank you'. It is typical for the juvenile to turn their frustrations and fears into anger towards the parent as the most readily available and safe object to attack. Thus it is necessary for a parent to understand that the backlash of negative emotions they receive for their efforts is not genuine in the sense that this is how the adolescent feels about them for ever but instead is a product of the emotionally charged situation.

An analogy would be the person who has a terrible day at work, comes home angry and vents their distress on their spouse in response to a trivial mistake that he or she has made. Teenagers are notorious for doing this towards their parents but usually lack the sophistication to recognize the unjustness of their actions or apologize later to the wronged parent. This does not mean that pointing this out to the adolescent will be beneficial. Instead such an action will most likely be met with denial and will only further aggravate the adolescent.

Acceptance of the unjust lashing out of the teenager at the time of the venting is probably the best option, and you can quietly reflect that you as a parent have served as a valuable resource by being there for them to reduce their level of anger and frustration. Listening without criticism is an art, and listening to an adolescent is perhaps one of the hardest arts to learn.

How to recognize when professional help is needed

Turning to a professional for help is necessary if the depression is so severe that it:

- Continues for more than a few weeks.

- Arises because of a topic that you are uncomfortable talking about.

- Has deteriorated to the point that they are considering suicide or the harm of others.

This is not a negative comment on your capabilities as a parent but instead a positive recognition that some subjects are just beyond the reach of parental interventions.

Therapists perform a vital service to children and adults by giving them a confidential setting in which to vent their feelings, examine their options and discuss coping strategies. The parent who seeks counselling for a depressed youth has not failed them but instead has recognized their needs and put the child's interests first in a most appropriate manner.

10. When Band-Aids Are Not Enough

A number of children engage in self-mutilation activities such as cutting their wrists or arms with knives, glass and paper clips. This behaviour is very confusing and frightening to parents who often assume that it is done in a suicidal manner. Some of the actions may have a suicidal motivation but the vast majority are not done for self-destructive reasons. Why then does a child want to self-inflict pain?

Logic suggests that hurting yourself is something people would try to avoid. Pain exists to let us know that something is wrong and that we need to perform an action to avoid or alleviate the pain. Thus when we sit on a tack we immediately jump up to prevent further pain. When we have grabbed something that is hot, we drop it so as not to cause further damage to our bodies. This same mechanism of avoidance exists in the youth who engages in self-mutilation and yet it fails to prevent the behaviour. Thus a deeper meaning must be sought if we are to understand and alter this perplexing problem.

In 2010 Patrick Kerr, Jennifer Muehlenkamp and James Turner wrote an excellent review in *The Journal of the American Board of Family Medicine* on the state of research into non-suicidal self-injury. There are multiple theoretical approaches to explaining the origins of and treating this complex problem, such as:

- Transference-focused psychotherapy.
- Metallization-based therapy.
- Manual assisted cognitive behavioural therapy.
- Dialectical behaviour therapy.

Common to all of these approaches are validation of the self-injurer's feelings (i.e. the non-judgmental acceptance of feelings) and the teaching of new skills. This latter concept of learning, developing and then applying new skills is especially applicable to parents when working with their children.

Some of the theoretical models of the origins of self-injury propose that there is an underlying personality disorder or other major psychiatric problem. In general, the behavioural approaches and social learning theories do not. There is not sufficient experimental data available at present to favour one approach over the others. Therefore let us consider how this harmful activity might begin, using the behavioural approaches.

The child who cuts himself repeatedly is not immune to pain. However, there is a mechanism that operates when we suffer an injury that involves the discharge of endorphins. These are natural pain-fighting chemicals that the body releases when it suffers an injury. They attach to the same pain receptors in the brain that powerful pain relievers such as morphine do, and in the same way alleviate the pain that we experience.

Let us look at a typical child who deliberately cuts his arm. Earlier in life he has done something that the parent has labelled as 'bad' and has been punished for his action. The punishment involved smacking by the parent as a form of discipline and since this involved the creation of pain there was a release of endorphins by the body as a coping mechanism. These went some way towards soothing the pain and also created a mild feeling of euphoria.

There then comes a time when the child is confronted by a situation in which he feels that he has done something wrong but no parental punishment occurs. Perhaps he has caused an argument between his parents over grades, betrayed a girlfriend by talking to another girl, or failed to be accepted on to the team that his parents expected.

He is then confronted by a situation that is difficult to solve. On the one hand he feels that he has done something wrong for which he should receive punishment. On the other there is little or no chance that the parent will react by smacking. Out of frustration a youngster may hit a wall with his fist, bang his head against something or even cut his arm or leg.

Such an action has two immediate consequences. The first is a relief of the emotional pain, for now he has received consequences for the supposed misbehaviour. He has thus 'paid his debt' in a manner of speaking. The second is the release of endorphins, which in turn creates the mildly pleasant internal feeling. These two effects can have a very powerful impact with the result that the next time he is feeling distressed because of some wrong he has committed, he is more likely to turn to self-harm as a way of coping.

Threatening a child who has started self-harming with further punishment (e.g. the infliction of pain) is generally unsuccessful in stopping the behaviour. Instead it is more likely to increase the self-abuse in the future. He or she will feel that the parents are confirming that they were indeed 'bad' and in need of punishment. It is necessary instead for the parent to sit with their child and determine the origins of the behaviour. When you both have a clear understanding of the precipitating event(s), only then can you help teach alternatives to self-inflicted pain.

In the situation where the parents have argued about their child's test scores, perhaps it needs to be explained to the child that there are things about him that precipitate conflicts and that these are the parents' responsibility to resolve and not his. In the example of him not making the team, the parental emphasis may be to explain that they want him to try his best, but that even when we try our best, sometimes it just isn't enough to succeed. When the conflict involves someone else such as a girlfriend or boyfriend, then the conversation might turn to a discussion of honour and actions that could be taken other than inflicting self-harm.

The commonality between all of these examples is something called re-framing. This means helping a young person to look at their behaviour in a new way or from a new angle. It is simply not enough to label the behaviour as wrong, even if you give an explanation such as 'self-abuse can cause serious scarring that will last a lifetime or can possibly even lead to death'. Such statements are sensible to an adult but have little or no meaning to a child.

It is necessary to explain the mechanisms involved in pain relief and how people wrongly learn to try and expunge guilt by inflicting self-harm. At the same time as doing this, the parent cannot simply leave the matter as it is or else the behaviour will continue. They must go on to explain how to think of the situation in a new way. Then they need to demonstrate how such a changed perception can lead to an altered outcome.

While the concept of reframing is relatively easy to state, it is sometimes difficult for people to grasp. In making a decision about situations involving moral dilemmas, by necessity people have to be selective in what, and how much, information they consider before coming to a conclusion about what is right and wrong. If we mull over too many alternatives it is easy to become overwhelmed with all the possible actions we could take.

However, youngsters have a tendency to consider a much more narrow range of information than most adults. Thus a significant part of what parents do in reframing a situation is to teach the contemplation of a larger range of facts. This may lead the child to a different conclusion than the previous one. By doing this, you are not negating the validity of the previous thinking of your child. Instead you are helping them to open their minds to a larger understanding of cause and effect.

There is one final piece to complete the puzzle of helping your child who has begun to inflict self-mutilation. This involves you as a parent finding alternatives to the use of physical punishment for misbehaviour. As discussed in previous chapters, role-modelling is a very powerful teaching mechanism. If you continue to use corporeal actions, there is a high probability that your child will imitate you.

REMEMBER THIS!!! Teaching that we should correct those mistakes that we can, but accept that we cannot always achieve what we want in life, is the quintessence of what it means to be a parent. This forgiveness of ourselves is a powerful thing to communicate and can have profound effects upon the attitude and behaviour of children. This is a lesson that will last a lifetime and parents are the best ones to instruct children in this belief.

A final note needs to be made about the suicidal individual. Some self-mutilation is not logical and instead involves questionable conclusions or actions based upon faulty thinking. In these cases the individual feels trapped by what seems to be an intolerable situation and the only way out is death. In these cases, the problem has deteriorated to the point that a parent can no longer deal with the child's actions and referral to a professional counsellor is needed.

If your youngster has indicated, even obliquely, that they are so frustrated that they would be better off dead then do not attempt to correct the situation yourself but immediately seek the assistance of a professional. In doing this you are being a responsible adult recognizing that nobody can be all things to somebody else. Once again, by this action you are helping your child to become a responsible adult.

11. What's Going On Here?

Children go through stages where they become opposi-
tional to their parents and other authority figures. When the
child is younger this is often felt by parents as a personal
rejection and a betrayal of their love and trust. It is necessary to closely examine what is going on in both the adult's
and the child's life in order to respond appropriately to the
defiance.

One common cause of a child becoming disobedient
is his or her parents separating or becoming involved with
other people. In such situations the child can be confused,
hurt and angry. He or she does not know how to respond,
for one parent may portray the other in very negative terms.

REMEMBER THIS!!! Your child needs to be kept out of the conflict
but not left out of the separation. Parents who
try to keep their separation 'civilized' and
refuse to talk to their youngster about why it has occurred
may inadvertently cause him or her to come to the conclusion that they are to blame. A child does not have the cognitive sophistication to be able to comprehend why parents
cannot continue to love or live with each other. The outcome may well be unfocused rebellion or defiance as a way
of expressing feelings of hurt and sadness.

When one parent takes on a new partner their former spouse will sometimes actively encourage disobedience from children as a way of obtaining revenge. Parents who do this tend to rationalize that all they are doing is trying to prevent 'that woman' or 'that man' (i.e. the new partner of their ex-spouse) from influencing *their* child. In such situations the juvenile feels torn loyalties and may become distrustful of adult veracity. Their young age means they are frequently incapable of comprehending what has happened to their lives. They do not understand the implications of their parent becoming involved with somebody else. A young person cannot understand that love between adults can change over time.

As a father or mother you need to come to the understanding that trying to protect your child from life changes and/or the use of the child for revenge purposes is unhealthy and ultimately destructive of your own parent–child relationship. Meetings with an independent third party such as a counsellor, pastor, court mediator, etc. are often beneficial. The focus of these sessions should be to help parents accept that the use of a child as a means of making the other adult angry ignores the destructiveness of their actions on the youth's emotional well-being. You will not enhance your own value in your child's eyes at the expense of the 'offending parent' but instead damage their ability to trust in *any* adult.

Another common cause of early childhood rebellion can be traced to parents who are trying to foster independence and resilience. Many parents believe that a child needs to be tough to stand up to all the societal pressures that are evident in our world. Therefore they will actively encourage their son to stand up to teachers who have given them too much work or a coach who has belittled their efforts. While there is nothing wrong with this idea in principle, the problem comes when the philosophy spreads from these specific incidents to other adults and eventually towards the parents themselves.

REMEMBER THIS!!! The pre-adolescent often lacks the ability to discriminate between appropriate and inappropriate times to stand up to others. In their mind the use of a particular mode of behaviour in one situation that has been approved by a parent gives them approval for *all* situations. Such generalization of rebellion does not indicate that there is something wrong with the child's thinking ability. Rather this is typical of most children and simply reflects the immaturity in the use of logical thinking that is a hallmark of childhood.

A third frequent type of rebellion is where it only appears that the child is being deliberately defiant of their parents. In such a situation, the son or daughter seems to have violated the precise instructions of their parents but in their mind they have complied with what they were told to do to the best of their ability.

CASE STUDY

Take for example the situation of a young girl whose parents worked on a military base, held high security clearances and did classified work. Her parents lectured her on never divulging to anyone what they did, for it might compromise their work. At the same time they had always told her about the importance of being respectful of those in authority above you and how necessary it was to follow orders.

At one point her teachers honoured her by selecting her to represent the school at a debating competition abroad. One of the routine requirements for participation was for her to complete a form talking about her home life, and specifically what her parents did for a living. When she told her teachers that she could not complete this part of the questionnaire she was told that she had to do so or else she could not compete and the school might well lose the competition.

Since she was in the school setting, and her teachers were those in 'authority' above her, she followed 'orders' and completed the questionnaire. The parents were furious at her when they were subsequently investigated by security forces for an apparent violation of their clearances by allowing information about their work to be revealed to a 'foreign entity'. The child's parents believed that she had deliberately disobeyed them when in her mind all she had done was follow instructions.

CASE STUDY

Another example of this was provided by a boy who was brought into the psychiatric centre by parents who were furious that he had thrown away the man's very expensive wedding ring.

The assumption was that the boy had some hidden anger towards them and was trying to punish or hurt the father by throwing something in the trash bin that had such enormous emotional value.

The boy was about age four and was confused and frightened by the reactions of his parents. He would not tell them what they had done that was deserving of such revenge. When he was separated from the parents and their accusations, he was able to give a very logical account of what had occurred.

Earlier the same day his mother had seen him take a bite of some old cake that had gone bad and that she had put in the bin. She scolded him for this and said that old things belong in the trash and were not to be taken out and eaten or used. She talked about germs and diseases and what others would think of somebody who wore old clothes or ate mouldy old food.

Later in the day he saw his dad's wedding ring on a table and recalled that when he had previously asked about it his father had said he had been given it a long time ago and well before the boy was born. Therefore, according to his logic, the ring was old; he had been told earlier that old things belong in the bin and thus followed the instructions of his mother and threw the ring away.

In this situation there was no desire for revenge or rebellion against his parents. Instead he had simply followed the instructions of his mother to the letter. As a consequence, rather than being praised for his good choices he had been berated for his apparent vengeful action.

The common resolution of these situations with young children lies first in accepting that a pre-teen simply does not reason in the same broad manner as an adult. Parents then need to clearly state what they expect of their child:

- Do you want your child to listen to all adults or just some? If it is just adults in certain situations then you must patiently list each one rather than assume that your child has the capacity to sort out which is right and which is wrong.

- You might try instructing your child to not do what they are told by an adult without first asking a second adult if it is okay.

Certainly these actions are more time-consuming than simply giving general rules but the rewards are usually worth the extra effort involved.

As the pre-teen moves into adolescence, his ability to reason like an adult and to make choices based on relativistic moral bases expands. At the same time, the adolescent enters a period of 'separation and individuation' and the formation of an 'independent adult identity'.

BACKGROUND INFO Nadine Medlin in a dissertation at the University of Nebraska-Lincoln summarized these developments well when she stated 'Psychological separation-individuation is the process by which the young adult renegotiates the parent–child relationship. The resolution of the identity crisis involves the synthesis of past and present, as the adolescent reintegrates the self in such a manner that allows the young adult to assume his or her place in society. Both processes are a vital part of the drive towards healthy personal adjustment.' Your child needs to become an adult by challenging, clarifying and finally adopting values that will last them a lifetime. Since parents are the most available source of these values, they can expect to receive the brunt of the apparent rebellion.

To accomplish these tasks successfully, many adolescents will initiate arguments with their parents, often for trivial reasons. This can be especially trying for adults since there seems to be no rhyme or reason behind the quarrels that occur. Attempts to reason with the rebellious adolescent almost always end in failure. This is due to the origins of the arguments, which have to do with the teenager developing two competencies:

- Sharpening their verbal skills to make their personal viewpoint known.

- Understanding that they are becoming an adult who can make independent decisions about their lives.

Neither of these necessarily has anything to do with solving problems or resolving conflicts, both of which tend to be the primary focus of parents.

Accepting that this is a necessary part of adolescence is hard for the average parent since typically we do not want our teenager to repeat our errors. We want to impart our experiential knowledge that we have had to endure so much frustration in our own lives to earn. However, making mistakes from poor judgements is a part of growing up; the job of parents is trying to prevent the decisions from permanently affecting the way life unfolds. Trying to force the adolescent to make the correct choice seldom works and usually only results in confrontation.

Additional causes of defiance in teenagers include:

- Depression.
- Lowered self-esteem.
- Anxiety.

These are all very typical feelings that adolescents struggle with during this turbulent developmental period. As a parent it is difficult to determine when the defiance of a teenager is part of their individuation process and when it is due to underlying emotional concerns. Rather than just react to the argument that your child initiates, it is much more fruitful and satisfying to talk with them, after everybody has had a chance to calm down, about why the conflict occurred.

When discussing the teenager's concerns, parents need to convey clearly that his or her feelings are normal in that most people struggle with such worries and upsets. You should try to help your child understand that you are on their side and are not the enemy. Instead of lashing out at you as a target on which to vent their frustrations you want them to view you as an ally in helping find solutions to their fears.

It is difficult for many parents to make the transition from giving orders or directives to giving suggestions and advice. Pre-adolescents are generally incapable of understanding such things as why pornography on a computer is something they should not view, or why a film that is rated above their age is inappropriate to see. As a parent you make the decision that the material is unsuitable and try to explain as best you can your reasons. However, the ultimate decision is yours; if your reasoned arguments fail to persuade, all you can do is choose what you think is the best course of action and hope that eventually they will understand your reasons.

When a child reaches adolescence such definitive prohibitions tend to fall on deaf ears. Your child wants to know *why* they cannot do something, such as go to a party at a friend's house whose parents are gone for the weekend. It is awkward at best for a parent to explain the innuendos involved in such a situation without directly accusing your child of inappropriate intent. Vague moral statements such as 'you might get into trouble' or 'something bad might happen' are not acceptable to the teenager.

It is necessary for the parent to think through their own feelings of unease before they respond. What is it that you really fear will occur at the other person's home? Is your child promiscuous and you are concerned about an unwanted pregnancy? Is there going to be drinking and/or drug-taking? Are these fears just a reflection of your own adolescent period?

 When you understand what it is that bothers you about your teenager engaging in an activity then honesty is advised. Clearly state your moral concerns and why you will not give your child permission to do something, but be aware that this does not mean that there will be unquestioned obedience. Most likely there will be protestations such as 'Well, I am *not* you' or 'You just don't understand!' However, if you have given reasoned and logical explanations that are consistent with your personal underlying beliefs then grudging compliance with your decision is much more likely. Even though the adolescent may argue to 'save face' they will accept the prohibition at a deeper level.

If you use a calm tone of voice, you have considered the desires and arguments of your child, and the principles underlying your decision are consistent with the family moral values, these things are usually much more important than the words themselves. You should try to remember that what you want your teenager to take away from the discussion is the *process* of decision-making that was followed. This is what will be remembered long after the party or film has been forgotten.

12. The Natives are Restless

'The teacher said that I need to have my son evaluated for ADHD. I think that they just want to put him on drugs to keep him quiet. But I don't want a zombie for a child, and I think that the problem is that they just don't know how to discipline kids any more!'

It is possible that at one point or another in your child's development, you or somebody else may question whether or not the youngster has ADHD. To ascertain whether this might be the case, parents often turn to the internet for information and find themselves subject to a bewildering array of opinions about the causes, cures and even existence of the condition.

It sometimes seems as though every person who has had any disagreement with the educational system has ventured an opinion about Attention Deficit/Hyperactivity Disorder and why it seems to be so prevalent in our society. Most research suggests that the problem affects some 3–5 per cent of children and is the most commonly diagnosed childhood behavioural disorder.

The ancient adage that knowledge is power is quite true when it comes to understanding the origins of and treatment options for ADHD and how to live with a youngster who has this condition. The first step is to develop an understanding of what the condition is and is not. Primarily, the diagnosis of a child as having an ADHD condition is a shorthand method of describing a cluster of symptoms. These symptoms are defined as problems in three basic areas: impulsivity, attentiveness and hyperactivity. For the condition to be diagnosed, these difficulties must continue for at least six months and interfere with academic, social or occupational functioning.

ADHD, predominantly inattentive type

The inattentive youth with ADHD may have problems focusing on topics that are inherently repetitive and not exciting. Thus your child may be easily distracted by almost anything when trying to learn their times tables or spelling but seem to be able to focus for hours on videogames. Videogames tend to be very fast moving and constantly evolving whereas the typical school lesson tends to impart ideas relatively slowly and logically. It is easy for the teacher or parent to believe that the child simply doesn't want to put in the effort to learn the lesson.

Certainly this is true of a number of children but in the case of the ADHD child he genuinely cannot focus his attention on the task at hand. Even when he tries to learn, he will find his mind wandering to such innocuous things as the sound of a bird outside the window, the laughter of somebody in the hallway or the antics of a hamster in a cage.

Differentiating between someone who truly has ADHD and one who is simply bored with a lesson is difficult. A parent needs to listen to their child's explanations for being sent to the headmaster so often or for poor performance.

Does the child say that the material is uninteresting and the subject is daft? Or has he tried to pay attention but just can't keep his mind on the topic? The difference is a subtle one that places the focus on something *inside* them as opposed to *outside*. This concept is one psychologists have labelled as 'locus of control'. If the focus is on something inside, this is one clue that there may be an ADHD difficulty.

 Individuals who truly have ADHD tend to display their difficulty in all subjects taught in and out of school, not just one. Situations requiring extended focusing, such as learning to tie knots in Scouts, reading instructions for a game or learning how to properly paddle a canoe are very frustrating for the person with ADHD despite the inherent fun involved in the activity. All of these are clues that there may be an underlying problem that is beyond their self-control.

ADHD, predominantly hyperactive type

In addition to the youngster who has a problem with focusing his attention, there is a second type of ADHD condition where the child must be in near-constant physical motion. He may be out of his seat every few seconds at school or tap his leg or pencil in an irritating manner. This tends to be a very big disruption in almost any classroom or setting requiring quiet and it is this child who is most often sent to the headmaster for disobedience. Punishment is ineffective since he really cannot sit still for more than a minute – or even just a few seconds – at a time. Children with this type of ADHD may absorb the lessons but just cannot remain physically still.

This does not mean that all children who make noises or wander around the classroom have ADHD. The difference is that the child who genuinely has an ADHD difficulty is more likely to understand what he or she should be doing but due to an internal 'drive' cannot remain still or successfully control the behaviour when reminded.

Nor should it be assumed that children with tics or repetitive single behaviours (e.g. pulling on their lips or hair, or snorting constantly) have ADHD; these behaviours often result instead from underlying anxiety states or sensory integration deficits. The differentiation between these problems and ADHD tends to lie in the pervasiveness of the behaviour for the ADHD child. Did the behaviour begin only at the start of the present term having never been displayed before? Is the problem only evident in one setting and not others? If either of these is true then the difficulty is probably not ADHD but instead may be situational anxiety.

ADHD combined type

In the third type of ADHD, known formally as ADHD Combined Type, the child has both the inability to physically remain still *and* the inability to focus for sustained periods of time. Usually the symptoms are not as extreme as in either of the other types. And since the problems tend to be more subtle, the diagnosing of the problem can be more difficult.

Parents may be able to readily identify concentration problems or difficulty remaining still at school or church, but what about when the child is at home? There the difficulty tends to manifest itself in such things as constant physical movement when watching a movie or playing a game. The child with focusing problems may find that they are uncomfortable if they are not constantly stimulated. Thus they may be playing a videogame while watching a movie and simultaneously have headphones on, listening to music.

 Any diagnosis of ADHD should only be made by a competent clinician after interviews with the child and the parents, and after obtaining testing and/or observational reports from others such as school personnel with extensive knowledge of the child's behaviour. Parents should not attempt to diagnose and treat the condition themselves, for similar symptoms can come from other conditions.

Examples of common problems which may result in ADHD-like behaviour are:

- Parental separations.
- Moving to a new town.
- Loss of a loved one.

Or, for that matter, anything that destabilizes the normal household routine. For the adolescent, falling in love can also lead to symptoms that look very much like an ADHD problem.

 What, then, causes a genuine ADHD condition to develop? The answer to this is that researchers still do not know the origins, although many theories have come and gone over the years. For example, at one point a major theoretical contender for understanding ADHD was that the condition was precipitated by fluorescent lights. The reasoning went that ADHD looks somewhat like a person who is having a mild seizure and seizures can be caused by intense flashing lights. Since fluorescent lights flash at the rate of 60 times per second and are found in many school settings, the assumption was made that the lights were causing ADHD.

When an experiment was conducted whereby the fluorescent lights in several schools were replaced with incandescent bulbs that do not cycle on and off, no change in the ADHD condition resulted and so the theory was disproven and abandoned. Similar cases have been made for refined sugar, artificial sweeteners, food dyes and poor parenting. All of these have been disproven or gone out of favour over the years, although there are still advocates of all of them that can be found on the internet.

Scolding or constantly punishing a child who has uncontrolled ADHD is ineffective and only results in frustration on the parent's part and further emotional problems for the child. A youngster with a true ADHD condition cannot help themselves in terms of focusing or sitting still. This is the way they are physically made and simply telling them to 'focus' or 'behave' does not work. They are usually aware that they act differently from their peers but cannot change voluntarily.

If your child is found to have an ADHD condition after a competent clinical evaluation then there are several treatment options that you as a parent can pursue. The use of medication is the easiest and most effective treatment. There are a number of different medications available, most of them being variants of a stimulant that increases the ability of the child to focus in school and reduces their hyperactivity.

Parents become concerned that the drug will make their child a zombie, or that the youngster may abuse the medication. Both of these are possible outcomes but only if you as a parent allow the child to be placed on too high a dosage or allow your older youth to have unchecked access to the pills.

When used appropriately, the medications tend to be very safe and to have few side effects. Those side effects that do occur, such as loss of appetite, tend to be temporary and are usually eliminated by adjusting the dosage or type of medicine that is given. And the benefits to the child, the parents, the household and the school all tend to far outweigh any side effects.

The medication tends to be effective within a day or two, with adults noting significant improvements in the child's ability to concentrate or remain in their seat. Children often report that they can pay better attention to what is going on in their classroom and are delighted at the improvement. There is a temptation at this point by parents to assume that the problem has been solved and therefore nothing else is needed on their part. Nothing could be further from the truth.

REMEMBER THIS!!! Once a youngster is receiving medicine then the parents must take over the responsibility for teaching the child to use his or her time appropriately. Teaching your child good study habits, establishing self-discipline for doing lessons and projects, and helping him to organize himself to get things done in an expedient manner are necessary. Simple things such as the following can assist the individual with ADHD in his learning:

- Turning off the TV and radio.

- Removing distracting toys and electronics from the work area.

- Making sure the study setting is well lit and tidy.

In the school setting, the parent can be an advocate for their child receiving extra time to take tests or even perhaps taking the test in a separate and less distracting environment from the rest of the class.

If you prefer not to use medication, there are behaviour modification programmes that have been created to help ADHD children. Usually these require development and monitoring by a qualified clinician, plus the cooperation of the parents and school together. These programmes tend to yield much slower results than the use of medication, and are most effective when the condition is of a mild to (at most) moderate severity.

 One crucial notion that a parent must keep in mind is that not addressing the problem and simply hoping that the situation will go away is a recipe for disaster. An untreated ADHD condition can lead to such things as:

- Failure in school.

- Ostracism from peers who are uncomfortable around a hyperactive child.

- A much lowered self-esteem, which may lead to depression or the development of a whole host of related psychological problems.

133

Parents should not believe that it is their fault that their child has this problem. However, neither should they just accept the condition as something untreatable.

Other developmental problems

In addition to the ADHD difficulty there are many other syndromes and problems which can predate birth. All parents want their children to be perfect in terms of physical and emotional development. Unfortunately it is a sad fact of life that despite mothers following a rigid diet during pregnancy, getting adequate amounts of rest and exercising regularly, a certain percentage of children are born with disabilities that affect their intellectual and behavioural functioning. The causes may sometimes be identified as chromosomal damage or recessive genes, but the majority of the time they are unknown, just as they are with ADHD.

The increasing array of medical tests available to parents during the early stages of a pregnancy has raised a significant challenge. A couple may have had ultrasounds and amniocenteses done and perhaps found that their baby will be born with a condition such as Down's Syndrome and thus have at least a mild level of mental retardation and a high probability of heart damage. They then face the agonizing choice of whether to abort the foetus or to give birth to a child that may need to be cared for throughout his or her lifetime by others. The choice is never easy to make, regardless of your religious orientation or personal feelings about abortion.

Parents who have given birth to a so-called 'special needs child', with or without warning, may face a choice between trying to raise the child at home and sending him or her to live in a specialized setting. Those who choose the former need to be cautious about the temptation to turn their decision into what can perhaps best be described as a crusade.

A number of parents succumb to the temptation to throw themselves and their families totally into the care of such children to the point that older siblings can end up inadvertently being robbed of a normal childhood. They are sacrificed to the care of their younger sibling.

Parents may focus so intensely on attending or leading support groups, or become so involved in raising money for research, that their crusade takes over the whole family focus. Older siblings who were once happy and normal children stop smiling and laughing and take on the aspect of premature adulthood. They may stoically put up with the destruction of their own toys by a sibling who has been identified as not being subject to the rules of the rest of the family. The family tends to treat the special needs child as though they were made of porcelain, with the perception that even a normal level of correction could somehow destroy or devastate them. Inappropriate behaviour is overlooked or excused by the parents due to their disability. The effect upon the siblings of the disabled child can be devastating.

Siblings can easily begin to believe that they exist not as an equal. Parents often remind older children that they need to take extra care of their brother for he is special and requires someone to look out for him. While this is objectively true, it ignores the need of every individual to feel that he or she is special in their own right, even if they do not have a handicap. No child should be made to feel that they are of lesser value than their brother or sister. Such actions by parents are unfortunate not only for the siblings whose lives are disrupted but also for the special needs child.

Correcting a special needs child with love and treating them as though they are normal and not broken or delicate is one of the most positive things a parent can do. In a family which includes a child with a disability, parents need to normalize the upbringing as much as possible. This does not mean that you ignore the disability but that you strive with the youngster to accept and adapt to it.

The use of the behaviour modification techniques described in earlier chapters is entirely appropriate with such children as long as the concepts are explained in terms consistent with their developmental level. As a parent you also have to be careful not to assume that what you would consider a positive reinforcer (see page 29) is the same as what your child finds pleasant or rewarding. An example would be physical contact.

Most children enjoy hugs and kisses but this is often not true of children suffering from autism spectrum disorders. For the autistic individual, hugs and kisses may be felt to be negative and may result in an avoidance of repeating the behaviour that you were trying to reward. Indeed, one of the most common early signs of autistic tendencies is a withdrawal from affection by others. Parents will seek help from professionals with complaints that their child arches his back when they are trying to hold him, or turns away when they reach for him. This tendency is part of the syndrome and not a personal rejection of the parent. For such children, the parents may find that they need to substitute other things for the physical contact in reinforcing behaviour, such as:

- Food.
- Toys.
- Music.

If the approach is individualized and the rest of the family's needs for attention and their own personal time are not ignored then raising a child with special needs can be as rewarding and fulfilling as any other.

13. Beyond the Birds and the Bees

Few things cause parents more worries than when their children display sexualized behaviour or reach an age when they begin to become interested in sexual activities with others. Parents become particularly concerned if this happens at a young age (below about age eleven): they note that their child seems to be masturbating or rubbing his or her genitals, or that they have developed a fascination with the genital areas of dolls or animals, and they fear that there may be something wrong.

Parents are often confused about whether these behaviours are in imitation of something that the child has been exposed to or something that they have just discovered on their own. The answer is that there are a number of children who simply discover the comfort of self-stimulation and it does not mean that they are deviant or have developed an unusually early sexual interest.

 To the young child the activity of rubbing oneself simply is a pleasurable act and does not have any sexual connotation. The sexual meaning of the gesture is something that an adult projects into the activity. If nothing in particular is done about the actions then usually they will fade away with the passage of time.

However, if the parent is distressed about the behaviour, or it occurs in a public place – which may cause other parents to not want their children to be around the masturbating child – then there are interventions that can be made to change the child's habits.

One response that parents typically attempt with a very young child is to try to localize the behaviour by saying such things as 'We don't do that around others! We only do that in the privacy of our bedroom or the loo!' The implication is that sexual behaviour should be confined to only certain areas and is not for public display.

This rarely works with the youngster, for the parent has misinterpreted the behaviour as being *sexual* in nature when it is not. Parents conclude that since the child is engaging in such an 'advanced' activity for his or her age that therefore he or she should be capable of understanding concepts like social embarrassment and privacy. From the child's perspective these ideas are very confusing. He or she does not have the cognitive capability or the developmental experience to understand such notions. The typical result is that the child develops a fear that he or she is being bad or doing something wrong when the parental intent was simply one of teaching the appropriate locale for the activity to take place.

What then can be done to address this behaviour if it has become a problem for the parent? One very successful technique is known as 'directed action'. This is simply the action of gently removing the child's hand from the area of attention without fanfare and redirecting it on to something that the child is fond of but which the parent feels is more acceptable, such as a toy or book. This is done without calling excessive attention to the masturbation by scolding, criticizing or yelling at the child. Instead it is something that is done as unobtrusively as possible.

Taking such action at the beginning of the activity before the pleasurable sensations have had time to be established usually results in the child learning quite easily not to masturbate. This is due to the fact that the substituted activity is more fun and interesting than the one that has been forestalled. If this is done consistently over time and across all situations in which the unwanted activity occurs then quite rapidly the offending behaviour dissipates.

A second action that parents can take to modify self-gratifying behaviour in the younger child is to use the concept of time-out (see page 35). Placing the child in an uninteresting environment every time the behaviour occurs creates an association in the child's mind between the two with the result that the pleasurable sensations he or she receives from doing the activity are more than counterbalanced by the negatives of being removed from a fun or exciting environment. This technique can be quite successful in eliminating the problematic behaviour if consistently applied. Parents sometimes object that the child will just continue with the self-gratifying action in the time-out setting but this rarely occurs, for the upset at being corrected tends to interfere with any idea of continuing the behaviour.

Unfortunately there is another possible explanation for the early display of sexual interests in young children. The sad reality of our society is that sexualized behaviour may be due to somebody having touched the youngster inappropriately. Possible perpetrators can range from another child all the way to an intimate family member.

If the child's actions in touching him- or herself can come from either self-discovery or the interference of another then how can the parent decide which is really happening so as to make the appropriate response? There is not a simple or complete answer to this conundrum. There are however some fairly straightforward things that the parent can do to help make an informed judgement.

 One thing parents can do is to note the timing of the behaviour: does it always occur after the child has spent time at a particular place or with a specific person (for example the home of a friend, relative or tutor)?

If the timing appears correlated with a certain person or situation then it can be seen as increasingly likely that the child's behaviour is linked to another person's actions rather than simply being self-discovery.

This does not mean that the person involved is necessarily a sexual deviant, for it may well be that the child has imitated something that he *observed* at the other person's house. Children often peek under doors and around corners and their natural tendency is to imitate what they observe adults doing with or to each other. This is especially true if it seems to be exciting or pleasurable. In addition there is the possibility that somebody else at the other household has introduced the sexual activities, such as a neighbour or even another child.

If you discover such an association then consulting a professional for help is recommended. This can be a psychologist, social worker, psychiatrist, or even the child's general medical doctor. It is prudent to do this sooner rather than later, for the sooner someone intervenes, in general the better the outcome. If there is a significant suspicion that someone has molested a child then intervening with the person in question may prevent other parents having to go through the same heartbreak that you experience.

Parents are often concerned about extended family relationships and wish to believe desperately that what has happened was either a one-off, an accidental encounter or the result of a temporary lapse in judgement. Most parents wish to believe the best of their relatives, friends and neighbours and often find that with the passage of time they feel that they can trust the perpetrator to be alone with their child again. This is unfortunate and can often lead to tragic results.

The statistics clearly indicate that the recidivism rate among perpetrators of such offences is very high. A review of the research literature by the Center for Sexual Offender Management by the US Department of Justice in 2001 found the following recidivism rates:

Perpetrator:	Recidivism percentage range
Incest offenders	4 to 10 per cent
Rapists	7 to 35 per cent
Child molesters (female victims)	10 to 29 per cent
Child molesters (male victims)	13 to 40 per cent
Exhibitionists	41 to 71 per cent

In addition, while you may be clear in your mind that the perpetrator has changed his or her behaviour, you must consider the import of the message conveyed by your action of allowing the other adult to be around your child. To your son or daughter you are in effect saying that what the other person did was okay. Although it may be stressful or create family arguments, the best course of action is to simply refuse to allow your youngster to be alone around the person ever again.

What should you do if another youngster is the perpetrator, or indeed if you learn that your child has been enacting such behaviour on another? Does this mean that they are deviant and must never be allowed around other children again? To address this concern you must first accept that a child may be doing something simply because they find it pleasurable and that they do not understand the *sexual* nature of the activity. Thus enacting this behaviour with other children is something that seems to them quite logical and reasonable and not something that is in any way 'wrong'.

Suppose that the behaviour is one they imitated after watching their parents or other adults engage in sex in real life or on television. Imitating this activity with another child (or doll or animal) may simply be repeating what they have seen. The action needs to be understood as an inappropriate behaviour that needs to be changed and not necessarily an indication of some sort of underlying perversion.

REMEMBER THIS!!! Inappropriate physical contact between siblings is something that occurs very frequently with young children. When siblings are fairly close in age they often bathe together, see each other in the nude and lack many of the social inhibitions that occur with strangers or friends.

Such activities as playing house, playing doctor and patient, etc. are common occurrences and can be easily interpreted as sexual in nature by parents, especially when the playing involves such things as:

- Kissing.
- Hugging.

- 'Examinations' of genital areas.
- Trying to have sex.

However, the children usually perceive such things to be normal based on the behaviour they have observed in others. Thus they are role-playing rather than doing something that is socially prohibited.

 To help the children amend their behaviour, tell them that their actions are not allowed and then describe for them the limits of what they *can* do when pretending to be a doctor, wife, husband, father, etc. Positive statements of what is acceptable, as opposed to simply listing what is unacceptable, generally generate better compliance.

Stopping further exposure to adult sexual activities is a necessary step, combined with a course of remedial action such as the use of the time-out technique described earlier. Close monitoring of your child around other children, especially siblings, is needed until the behaviour has been completely extinguished. The other children who have participated with your child also need similar interventions to stop the behaviour from reverberating back and forth or spreading to new groups of children.

After about the age of eleven, the nature of sexual interactions takes on a new meaning. As the child enters puberty and develops a more adult-like social understanding of sexual actions, they start to perceive their earlier experiences in a different light and see touching, hugs, kisses and cuddles as having genuine sexual connotations.

Someone who was molested as a child by an older individual will now comprehend the experience as a sexual exploitation. Even if they resolved the abuse through therapy and appropriate parental responses, they will often have to process the event again with this new insight into what the actions really meant. This can be very troubling and confusing to parents who have lived through the trauma once already and thought that they had it resolved and behind them. They now find themselves having to work through their own and the child's trauma all over again.

Although this does not arise with everyone who has been abused sexually, it is such a common occurrence that parents are well advised to be prepared for it. One way to prepare is to keep very good records of exactly what happened at the time of the original abuse, what they as parents did and did not do, and why. Resuming counselling for a short period of time is sometimes needed when this stage of the young person's development is reached.

At about this same period of growth, parents often find that their children stop engaging in actions that they have taken for granted as being a normal part of the parent–child relationship. These might be such things as:

- Kissing goodnight.

- Walking into a bathroom when the parent is in the shower or bath.

- Allowing the parent to assist with dressing or the fitting of bras, etc.

- Holding hands.

- Engaging in physical horseplay.

Almost all adolescents, not just those who have been abused earlier in life, tend to start reading sexual innuendos into such activities even when there is absolutely no basis in reality for such an interpretation. Many parents find themselves falsely accused of being 'homosexual' or of wanting to sexually abuse their child even when this was never the parent's intent.

If this happens, instead of reacting with righteous indignation, it is much more productive to calmly talk with your teenager about their feelings and to reassure them that such was not your intent. The adolescent is struggling to define themselves in terms of the new urges, desires and feelings that they are experiencing and parents need to understand that this is a normal part of growing up.

As the adolescent develops physically into a mature individual, parents often find that they have a difficult time accepting the idea of their child now becoming an adult. They are reluctant to relinquish the parental control that they once had over their entire life's activities and thus the stage for conflict is set. For example, birth control devices such as pills for females or condoms for males can provoke a serious dilemma for the parent. If you provide these to your child, are you effectively giving them permission to engage in sexual activities with peers or are you just being a responsible adult and trying to prevent unwanted pregnancies?

REMEMBER THIS!!! The choice to either provide or deny these things needs to be made on solid religious, moral and philosophical grounds that are clearly and repeatedly discussed with the teenager. Many parents have tried to use the provision or withholding of such things as a way of exerting control or punishment for behaviour that they feel is undesirable. Such actions almost always backfire in that the adolescent views the parent as being dictatorial and arbitrary, and therefore feels more inclined to do the opposite of what the parent wants.

As discussed previously, to the adolescent, the feelings and urges that they experience with the flood of new hormones into their system are unique and unprecedented. Despite their paying lip-service to the idea that others have indeed felt love deeply or had similar intense drives, they harbour a suspicion that this is something that only they have ever experienced. Therefore advice from parents on how to act with members of the opposite sex is often ignored because the parent 'has no idea how the teenager really feels'.

REMEMBER THIS!!! Deciding to engage in sexual relations with a peer is often done not to defy the parent but because of the perceived depth of feeling that they have towards the one they love, or the importance to their own social standing of being sexually active. Therefore it is important that when parents approach the topic of sexual interactions with others they do so with this understanding of the adolescent psyche in mind. If the parent simply tries to reason with the teenager as an equal and gives advice based on their own life experiences then most likely their suggestions will be disregarded as irrelevant.

Sexual relations that are voluntarily engaged in by adolescents are subject to a number of influences, such as:

- The activities of peers.

- Role models in popular culture.

- The activities of parents and relatives.

- Hormones.

- Moral commitments such as to religious organizations.

- The teenager's perceived level of emotional attraction to the potential partner.

Complicating the parent's job in talking with their teenager is that the relative strength of each of these influences waxes and wanes depending upon multiple factors, such as:

- Their age.

- Loneliness.

- Popularity.

- Having friends around with whom they can discuss their concerns.

- Emotional events happening in their lives such as parental divorce.

It is thus almost impossible to try to fathom all the things that are pressuring a youth to have or not have intercourse at a given time. However, this does not mean that parents should just give up on talking about this important area of development. Instead they must take a step back from day-by-day life and try to respond to a broader moral picture of what it is that is important to them in their teenager's behaviour.

At what age do you believe it is permissible for an adolescent to engage in intercourse with another? Most parents would prefer never to have to address this issue for it has so many conflicting moral implications that it is one that we have rarely addressed in relation to ourselves let alone our children.

The stereotypical response of many parents is 'when they get married' or 'after they have grown up'. Although this seems to solve the problem, in reality it only creates further dilemmas. The typical adolescent most often feels that they are already mature or 'grown up' when it comes to this area of their lives and capable of making their own decisions.

Instead of coming up with a definite age at which it is acceptable to have sex with another individual, it is perhaps more productive for the parent to ask the teen what they think is appropriate and desirable. Parents most often balk at this idea for they assume that their son or daughter will respond with a statement such as 'immediately', when in reality this rarely occurs.

Teenagers generally are very appreciative of being asked for their opinion on such an important 'adult' topic and usually respond with either thoughtful suggestions or a confused response such as they do not know. In either case, you now have an opening to talk to your child about this critical area of their development.

The resulting discussion needs to be wide-ranging and not just limited to simple statements about ages at which you can begin having sex. The discussion should cover multiple topics:

- Pregnancy.

- Venereal disease.

- Responsibility.

- Allowed or disallowed actions consistent with your family's moral beliefs (e.g. living with someone to whom you are not married).

Typical questions that need to be explored are:

- What are your beliefs about the age differences between people who have intercourse?

- What are your thoughts concerning oral and anal sexual activities?

- How long do relationships last when an unplanned or unwanted baby is the result of the interaction?

- What values do you hold about multiple partners, homosexuality, casual sex and sexual relations outside of or in addition to marriage?

The list of topics to be discussed is large and obviously a single session is not enough. This should be an ongoing discussion that you return to as the adolescent matures and as their needs change.

At the same time as having these discussions, you must consider carefully the impact of your own behaviour upon your child. As a role model to them, it is almost inevitable that you will have a significant impact upon their actions if you do the following:

- Engage in an affair outside of your marriage.

- Live with another person to whom you are not married.

- Have sexual relations with multiple partners.

- Watch explicit movies or shows with a sexual content.

Children of all ages are much more likely to 'do as I do' rather than simply 'do as I say'.

A discussion of sexual values and practices with your adolescent does not mean that you will always agree with each other but at the very least you will begin to understand and respect each other's reasoning. Any fixed ideas regarding how your child will ultimately think and behave in this important area may still need to be modified, but addressing the issues in this way gives you a better chance of imparting your desired outlook than if you leave it to chance. Rarely will anyone else do this for you (a school or church, say) and even more rarely will your child develop these ideals on their own.

Discussions with teenagers on such emotionally laden topics as sex are never easy. You should expect tears (from both of you), anger and frustration. However, if you are to have any chance at all of influencing your child's development then you must persevere.

What should a parent do if their adolescent questions his or her own sexual orientation and believes that he or she is either homosexual or bisexual? When signs, symptoms or overt evidence of such proclivities occur, they should be addressed by a frank and open discussion with the teenager. Being an adolescent is almost synonymous with the idea of defining who and what you are as a person. The teen is unclear as to what values he should hold dear and what beliefs to carry on into adulthood. Questioning one's sexual orientation is a typical part of this process and should be recognized as such by the parent.

REMEMBER THIS!!! Homosexuality, according to the results of most research, is not a 'lifestyle choice' but either biologically determined or, occasionally, a reaction to trauma. Parents may initially be unhappy at the thought of having a gay son or daughter, but a genetically determined condition cannot be changed by all the parental screaming, pleading or threats in the world. Thus homosexuality should be viewed by parents as something inherent in the nature of the child.

In the case of inherent homosexuality, the purpose of seeking assistance from a counsellor should be to help the family become comfortable with their child's sexual orientation and *not* to change this orientation. This is a subject of tremendous emotional import to both the parents and youngster, with family therapy perhaps being the best approach to gain acceptance by all.

Trauma-induced or reactive homosexuality is a reaction of the teenager who is caught between the biological drive to want to experience a sexual life and the negative connotations of some severe past experiences. A classic example would be a girl who was regularly and forcefully sexually abused by a male for a period of months or years prior to becoming a teenager. Now that she is an adolescent and understands the nature of what has been happening, she is at one and the same time repulsed by the thought of sex with a male due to the abuse but wanting to experience the closeness, love and acceptance of a sexual relationship. The natural object on whom she bestows her affections might therefore be another female.

In such a situation, the individual needs psychotherapy to learn to cope with what has happened to her with the supportive involvement of the parents. With such help she may or may not retain her homosexual orientation. This is dependent upon a very wide variety of factors, such as the intensity of the abuse and the nature and depth of the attachments she has formed, as well as the reactions of others around her.

In either case in which the youngster turns out to be gay or bisexual, it is necessary for the parents to examine once again their own value systems of what is and is not important to them in their offspring. To have a child with a homosexual orientation is *not* the end of the world. Acceptance of the adolescent for who they are is the key; condemnation of them or an attempt to bully them into becoming what you want will only drive them away.

A parent who becomes obsessed with the sexual orientation of their child may end up destroying any validity in their child's eyes of the other values that they have tried to impart, such as honesty, lovingness, sensitivity and responsibility.

The parent communicating their own true feelings without condemnation and openly listening to the child's concerns is the foundation upon which acceptance is built. The process is slow and may sometimes require the assistance of a counsellor but the eventual result in terms of the lifelong relationship with your son or daughter is well worth the effort.

14. Dangerous Frontiers at Home

Of all the changes over the past 30 years that have affected the behaviour of children and childrearing practices, the internet must rank near the top for both pervasiveness and intensity. The parent who ignores this medium of communication and social influence does so at his or her peril.

Hardly a day goes by without the popular media relating a story of an internet predator that has succeeded in seducing a youth into sexual activities or an inappropriate relationship. In many ways the internet is like the old Wild West in that it is a place full of mystery, almost unlimited potential and yet deadly danger for the unwary. The internet and related online and offline gaming can exert both a positive and a negative influence over the development of children of all ages. If you are to have any chance of rearing your child in a manner reflecting your values and ideals then you must give considerable thought to the following:

- The sites that your child is allowed to visit.
- The e-mail contacts they can have.
- The games they are allowed to play.

With the pre-adolescent child, perhaps the biggest influence on their moral development comes from the games you allow them to play. Before you decide to let your child play a game you need to decide what are the core values that you hold dear. There are games that glorify stealing, hurting others and killing. There are those that treat men and women as sex objects that are there to be used. Then there are those games that portray loyalty to peers or gangs as being above society.

USEFUL TIP Simply following a rating code on the game will not give you a true sense of the values represented in the game. If you have decided to allow your child to participate in computer games on the internet or those available offline then it is necessary that you play the game at least once to gain an insight into what moral values are being promoted.

You should approach the game with a view of the moral values taught:

- Is stealing and the acquisition of wealth or power valued above all else?

- Does the game involve cutting enemies to pieces, with blood and gore flying everywhere?

- What messages does it send out about respect for the property and rights of others?

If the answers to these queries are not what you desire then no matter how popular the game, it should not be played by your child.

Too often we tend to unquestioningly accept that games are a fantasy world that can be clearly distinguished as separate from everyday reality. The truth is that children make little distinction between the two. The role model of a parent going to work every day to provide for their family, saving for the future and being responsible is unfortunately accepted at best as equal to the violent hero of a videogame – and often much lesser in the eyes of a child. Children do not have the wealth of experience of the adult to distinguish between reality and fantasy.

Internet pornography

Most users of the internet are aware that there are pornographic sites readily accessible. The developers of these sites often wish to normalize their own perceptions of sexual interactions by involving as many others in their activities as they can. When this is done they can then rationalize that 'everybody does it so it must be okay'. Some people will readily make such sites accessible to children, and can be quite ingenious in how they do this. Therefore as a parent there are two main things that you must do concerning these sites:

- Block as many destructive or disturbing sites as possible from your computer while periodically reviewing what your child is accessing.

- Hold frank and open discussions with your child about the nature of what they have viewed and which activities are, and are not, appropriate.

It is not enough to simply prevent the exposure of your child to negative sexual or moral role models. You must present the positive alternative in terms of your own beliefs and standards that you wish your child to emulate.

This presents a quandary for many parents. Adults often hold the idea that there should be one set of moral standards for adults and another for their children. Many parents today use the internet for cybersex. Their rationale is that such activities do not violate their vows to be faithful to their significant other because after all there is nothing real about the sexual activity and therefore where's the harm?

In a similar manner parents feel that as an adult they can engage in 'harmless' role-playing computer games in which they steal, lie, kill or maim without problem since they can distinguish clearly between fantasy and reality. The belief system is that they will not blur the lines between what they do for 'fun' and what is real.

As adults we believe we have the wisdom to choose limits to our behaviour, to which we stringently adhere, and this is the difference between a child or teenager going to the site and ourselves. While not debating the merits of this argument, I would again suggest that you must examine the effect your actions have upon the developing mind of a young person.

If you smoke, you increase dramatically the probability that your child will smoke. If you drink then you increase the probability that your teen will consume alcohol. Imitation of what adults do rather than what they say is a fact of life.

Thus if you go to such sites it becomes much more likely that your child will do so too.

Is it not possible to hide such activities from your children? It's unlikely. There are legions of parents who can attest to the sad fact that children tend to be more computer literate than their parents, and their ability to access what you have been viewing is quite amazing.

If the morals of the games and sexual sites are such that you would find it disturbing if your youngster should visit them, then you need to reconsider your own actions. Being a responsible parental role model is not easy. However, the reward of pride in a child who displays our treasured values of honesty, truthfulness and caring is incalculable.

Adolescents and the internet

For the somewhat older child, and especially the adolescent, chat rooms and social networking sites seem to be an ever-increasing source of social activity. Such sites allow the shy child to be bold without immediate consequences. There is the appearance of intimacy without having to deal with the awkward silences and embarrassments that face-to-face meetings entail.

Chat rooms provide the opportunity to exaggerate your age, experience, looks, interests, etc. in such interactions without being called to account. You can adopt alternate personas apparently without consequence or cost. Unfortunately such activities also tend to leave a child who is struggling with the developmental questions of

163

who they really are vulnerable to manipulation, abuse and exploitation.

Adolescents have used sites to ridicule their peers in the name of a harmless prank or joke. Older individuals have found access to younger and more malleable minds that can be shaped to fit their own ideas of love and acceptance. Sexual predators are infamous for their ability to say anything and everything an adolescent or child wishes to hear in order to obtain access to a new victim.

 It is not simply enough to try to prohibit such activities, for devices capable of providing internet access – whether computers or smartphones – have become utterly ubiquitous. Instead it is once again necessary that you talk openly and honestly with your son or daughter about their activities on the internet and emphasize that they are connecting with real people and not just computer-generated characters.

As a parent you must caution your child about what activities people may try with them and also monitor what it is they are saying to others. This does not mean that you must view every e-mail your child sends out, or review every conversation they hold in a chat room. However, you can and should create the expectation that all such activities are subject to parental review.

Parents often recoil at the idea that what their child says and does on the internet or in text messages should be subject to parental review. They protest that this violates basic rights of privacy. While this is a noble idea, unfortunately it is also nonsense. Tens of thousands of people have found to their dismay that what they thought was a private and sometimes intimate conversation on a computer at work is legally subject to the review of company security people.

Most activities on a computer can be accessed by others, as the hordes of hackers who steal identities, financial data and personal files can attest. In a work setting involving computers you do not have any privacy rights. Why, then, should you try to convey to your child that somehow their data is sacred when this is so obviously false? It would be better to create the perception that what they say and do can, and probably will, be reviewed by somebody else. This other person should logically be a parent and thus from the start your child should not be writing or saying things that they would not want you to hear.

This is the reality that we live in today and all you are doing is teaching your child to accept the world as it is. Our lives are increasingly under constant observation from speed cameras that record our driving habits to closed-circuit TV viewing of banks, car parks and intersections. We need to accept that others have access to our personal habits and activities, and if we do not like what others might see about us then it is our activities that will have to change, not the monitoring.

15. Is That the Headmaster Calling Again?

Upon the subject of education, not presuming to dictate any plan or system respecting it, I can only say that I view it as the most important subject which we as a people may be engaged in.

—Abraham Lincoln

Parents tend to invest a lot of emotional energy into their children's activities at school. Some parents see a good education as the ticket to a better way of life. Others view school as the opportunity to demonstrate their child's sporting prowess and become that star athlete that they always wished they could have been. Then there are the parents for whom school exists to make the social connections that they feel are necessary for their youngster to succeed in life.

Thus when a child begins to fail at school, parents usually take it very personally, as though the child has deliberately defied them or is wasting an opportunity that they would give almost anything to have back for themselves. The stereotypical parental response is one of anger that is usually directed at the child but many times at the teacher or school for their failure to sort out the problem.

Parents, with a lot of justification, feel that they have their hands full with their own responsibilities of work, paying bills and running the household. There are many individual reasons for poor school performance but they can usually be broken down into a few comprehensive categories. These include:

- Learning problems inherent in the child.
- Emotional difficulties.
- Social or relationship problems.
- Reactions to the household.

If you as a parent are to assist your youngster in achieving success at school it is essential that you determine the underlying reasons behind the failure.

While this seems logical and reasonable, unfortunately many parents ignore this simple concept and assume that their child has simply stopped putting in the effort to succeed. From this belief there follows an idea that what is needed is to enforce proper discipline by restricting activities or promising rewards for good grades.

Occasionally this works, for children can become as lax as any adult in doing work and sometimes all they need is an increase in outside incentives to increase their efforts and succeed. However, parents can become fixated on this as the only approach, with the unfortunate result that the other potential causes of school failure are ignored.

How, then, should a parent respond to the news that their son or daughter is not succeeding at school? The first action should be to make sure that there are no physical reasons for the problem. Schools tend to do a very good job at vision and hearing screenings but they are not perfect. A screening that was normal at, say, age six does not necessarily mean that at age ten they will not need glasses or have a hearing problem. Having these things evaluated is very easily done. If you fail to do this then ask yourself how you would feel if, after six months of constantly restricting activities and giving extra chores for poor performance, you find that the problem is that they cannot read or see the board due to a need for glasses?

Once physical causes have been ruled out then the parent needs to determine the parameters surrounding the problem:

- Is your child experiencing failure in all areas or only a few?

- Is the problem located at home in terms of completing homework assignments or does it happen only at school?

This is where consultations with the teacher, headmaster, guidance counsellors, school nurse, etc. can prove invaluable. These people are professionals and you should listen carefully and without bias to what they have to say.

If the problem seems to be occurring exclusively or mostly at school then a specific learning disability or developmental problem may be the difficulty. These can encompass such things as:

- A block or deficiency in the ability to learn in a particular area (e.g. in reading, mathematics, writing, etc.).

- An overall lack of capability (e.g. due to mental retardation or developmental delay).

- The effects of a physical condition (e.g. ADHD, an autistic spectrum disorder, seizures).

- A result of emotional problems (e.g. depression, anxiety, hearing voices, etc.).

Most educational systems have access to school psychologists who can determine through testing if there is a specific learning disability (i.e. an internal block to being able to learn at a typical rate) or capability problem.

If you suspect a disability is the problem then becoming an advocate for your child to be thoroughly evaluated is appropriate. If a learning disability or intellectual deficit problem is diagnosed then specialized teaching techniques can be adopted into the school setting that will aid your child in their learning. The teachers who apply these techniques are called special education teachers and the students usually learn with them for one or two hours per day, with the rest of the day being spent with the regular classroom.

As a parent of a 'special needs child' you can learn ways of instructing, understanding and interacting with your child at home from these teachers.

Even if the evaluation results are negative for a learning disability, mental retardation or physical problem with your child, the evaluation team at your school will almost always venture opinions that offer insights into the reasons for the difficulties your child is having.

Let us assume that the psychological evaluation has been completed and there is not an intellectual or learning problem that will explain the school failure. If this is the case then there are three main possibilities:

- That there is an emotional or psychological problem that has interfered with the child's ability to perform at an acceptable level in the school setting.

- That some sort of social problem has caused the difficulty.

- That their poor performance is a way of the child getting back at a parent or a way of expressing their anger or frustration.

Emotional or psychological problems that affect a child can range from depression or anxiety at a temporary situation at home (e.g. the parent has lost their job and the family's future is uncertain) to severe psychiatric conditions of auditory and visual hallucinations. In many ways, how the child is getting on at school can be viewed as a weather vane by which the parent can gauge the child's overall general adjustment. In the cases of depression and anxiety, the interventions discussed earlier (see chapter 9) are appropriate, while with the more severe psychiatric conditions, professional treatment is needed involving the whole family. However, if the failure at school is due to social problems then the situation becomes even more complicated for the parent.

The school setting is most often the primary one for your child to learn how to interact with others. It is in this setting that he will learn how to cope with bullying and dominance issues and to form friendships (and likewise to make enemies). Parents tend to think of school as a place to acquire learning. To a young person, however, the social aspects of school are as important, and often more important, than the actual instruction that occurs.

Perhaps your youngster is feeling left out of a clique to which they want to belong, or does not believe that they have any friends. Perhaps they are ashamed of how they look. If these or other social issues are distressing your child and they cannot figure out how to cope with them then how can you expect them to give priority to finishing the English assignment they have been given or work on improving grades?

The only real way to determine that your child has acceptance or social coping issues is to

172

really talk with them about their school activities and experiences. This does not mean you ask your child how their day went at school and when they reply with the typical 'okay' that you accept it. Instead it means that you listen to the subjects that they bring up and the words that they use. You must pay particular attention to the adjectives with which they describe others (words like 'hateful', 'bullying' and 'mean' should set alarm bells ringing) as you engage them in a genuine conversation about what has been happening at school.

You might try talking about how to cope with bullies, jealous rivals or friends who seem to betray confidences. Children are very sensitive to rejection and giving suggestions as to ways to behave around others so as to make friends can be very helpful. Do not succumb to the false assumption that your words of encouragement or examples of how you dealt with a similar problem when you were younger are falling upon deaf ears. Although children rarely reveal the true effect of what you suggest, the reality is that your conversations are probably having a very significant impact.

When a child feels secure about who and what they are relative to their peers then an improvement in grades often follows, although it does take some time.

What about the situation where there are no indicators of emotional or social problems interfering with your child's performance in school? Let us assume that you have consulted your doctor and the school psychologist and talked with your child about what is going on at school and in their social life. Despite all of these actions you have found nothing that would account for the general deterioration in grades.

In this situation it becomes probable that the child is deliberately underperforming for reasons that probably have very little to do with the school subject matter. Although it is very difficult, you must avoid the trap of just responding with anger and hurt. Instead you must attempt to dispassionately analyse the situation as though you were a disinterested outside observer. You must determine:

- When did the behaviour start?

- What was going on in the family at the time?

- What has been the result of the child's actions?

The situation of a ten-year-old girl who came to therapy because of parental concerns about poor school performance is typical of many children. There were no physical causes for her behaviour and the results of the psychological evaluation suggested somebody whose potential for achievement was well above the grades she was receiving. No emotional disturbance problems came to light. Neither she nor her parents could identify any social concerns which might account for the deterioration in her grades from being an excellent student down to at best a low average student.

Her parents had tried setting up a system of rewards for good academic achievement, with no success. They had then tried to restrict her activities so that she would spend more time completing her assignments, and again observed only marginal improvement. Despite them spending hours with her at home and making sure that the assignments were completed, the daughter never seemed to turn them in to the teacher. In desperation they turned to a counsellor to try to understand what was happening.

As this young lady talked it became apparent that there had been very gradual and significant changes in the family dynamics. The family was composed of the two parents, who had a stable relationship with no separations or substantial ongoing conflicts, the ten-year-old daughter and her eight-year-old brother.

The daughter had always done exceptionally well in school, while the son was at best a mediocre student who required a lot of assistance from his parents. However, his one area of strength and parental pride was in sports and he was involved in a number of structured activities requiring a lot of time and effort on the part of the parents. The parents rationalized to themselves that the extra time they had to spend with their son and their involvement in his sporting activities was necessary to build his self-esteem. All of this was true, but ignored the fact that they were dealing with a ten-year-old who did not reason the same way that they did.

To the daughter, the attention that the parents lavished on the son was a direct loss to her of time and love. When she excelled in school the parents spent even less time with her, for they did not have to spend hours with her completing her activities as they did with their son. However, when she began losing or not completing her assignments and her grades began to fall, and the calls and notes from her teachers became more frequent, the parents spent ever-increasing amounts of time with her to make sure that missing assignments were finished and that she completed the new ones.

There is an old saying among psychologists: bad attention is better than no attention at all. Thus the amount of time that her parents spent with her doing schoolwork more than made up for the emotional cost of being criticized. The result was that her grades continued to fall despite all their efforts.

In solving this situation it was important that the parents understood that time and attention from them was reinforcing to the daughter. Once this was done, the parents were able to identify activities that they could do with the daughter that were specific only to her and not the son. By carefully balancing the needs of both children for time and attention the family was able to establish a relationship where the daughter did not feel slighted by the time that was spent with the son. In a relatively short time her grades improved dramatically.

School refusal

A final difficulty that needs to be mentioned in relation to performance at school is a situation identified as early as 1941 and originally called 'school phobia' but now labelled 'school refusal'. A review of the research literature by Wanda Fremont in 2003 suggests that this condition affects from 1 to 5 per cent of all children. If untreated there is a significantly increased risk of developing long-term psychiatric disorders later in life.

The name suggests that the child is afraid of the school situation for some reason and thus becomes ever more anxious as they approach the school setting. However, rarely is there fear of the school itself. Instead there tend to be two subsets of this anxiety disorder that need to be recognized:

- Where there is something or someone at school that the child is afraid of encountering.

- Where the child is afraid of being away from the home environment.

Both of these problems can result in a fear surrounding going to school.

In the first situation the fear can result from such things as bullies or groups that tend to exclude the child. Adults avoid situations which make them uncomfortable and children react the same way. Perhaps the major distinction between children and adults is the tendency of youngsters to not display or recognize their fear for what it is and instead to express the fear as anger. Older children will often say that they just don't want to go to school and become enraged when you try to enquire as to why they do not.

As a parent you must listen for the message inside what your child is saying rather than the surface communication:

- Is their display of anger about school totally out of proportion to the stated cause?

- Is it out of character for how they usually react to situations?

If so then most likely their anger is actually a manifestation of fear or anxiety.

Talking with your child about what it is that they fear and then discussing ways to cope will go a lot further towards resolving the situation than logical arguments about the need for going to school or the value of an education. This is a situation that offers the parent the chance to teach how to handle intimidating people or groups and should be seized.

In the second subset of school refusals, where the youngster is experiencing a sense of fear concerning their situation at home, the child misses school because he or she does not want to be away from the home setting. Typical problems where this may arise include parents who are arguing constantly and are on the verge of separating or divorcing. Other examples would be when a parent is engaging in an affair that the child has learned about or a family financial crisis that threatens to disrupt the ability of the family to stay together. Another typical concern is the absence or potential absence of a family member due to such things as impending military deployment.

Any of these situations can create a loss of security and trust in the home environment on the part of the child. They may want to stay around the house in the vague belief that if they are physically present that somehow they may be able to prevent the household from falling apart. As a parent you know that this is not so.

Almost all children need a safe base from which to venture forth. If the safety and security of the home is threatened then the ability to leave the home for such an activity as going to school is severely impaired. Thus children may talk about a fear of school but the school refusal is really due to a perception of a family catastrophe if they are gone from the home.

Resolution of the home conflict is therefore necessary to address the school refusal. When you resolve the deterioration in the home setting it is highly probable that difficulties with school attendance will rapidly dissipate. Family discussions involving the child are often beneficial. Children constantly surprise parents who do this with their suggestions for sensible and reasonable actions.

If the school refusal does not respond to parental intervention then seeking the assistance of a counsellor is advised. Treatment using such techniques as cognitive behavioural modification or systematic desensitization is very effective in resolving these anxieties. The success rate has been estimated by researchers to be about 80 per cent.

16. When it all goes Pear-shaped

Divorce is one of the ugliest words in the English language. The termination of a marriage is destructive to individuals, couples and families. However, it is a fact of life that perhaps as many as half of all marital relationships currently end in divorce. People have tried to avoid this event by simply living with their partner without getting married, but this ruse does not avoid the pain of the break-up on all individuals involved. Although I do not know of a way to make a divorce (and this term I will also use to cover live-in relationships) totally painless, there are multiple things that can be done to reduce the disruption to everyone.

Relationships can end for many reasons, with the most common being:

- Affairs on the part of one or both partners.

- A loss of, or deterioration in, the love you once felt.

- Physical/emotional abuse or neglect.

- Addictions to drugs, alcohol, pornographic material, etc.

- A desire on the part of one or both partners to 'be free' and pursue a perceived lost lifestyle.

All of these situations share the commonality of negative feelings towards someone you once loved or believed that you loved.

Parental affairs

In the situation where you or your partner has had an affair there are often feelings of guilt, shame and regret. When people find themselves falling in love with someone else and decide that the current relationship cannot continue, they often engage in a mental mechanism first postulated in 1957 by Leon Festinger and labelled 'cognitive dissonance'. In this situation they tend to emphasize the positives of their new love and downplay his or her negatives, while doing the opposite with their spouse. This mental activity makes it easier to justify their being unfaithful to a previously committed relationship.

It is perhaps easiest to see this activity occurring in the purchase of an object, such as a new car. Let us assume that you have narrowed your choices down to two models that are similar in price, say, a Vauxhall and a Ford. Each has some positives and some negatives compared to the other. After agonizing over the choice you finally opt for the Vauxhall and immediately cognitive dissonance starts. As you become committed to the choice you find yourself recalling all the positives of the model you are getting and the negatives of the one you rejected. At the same time you downplay both the negatives of the one you chose and the positives of the one rejected. The result is happiness with your choice.

If this were the end of the situation all would be well. However, cognitive dissonance has another side to it that engages *after* the choice has been made. Following the

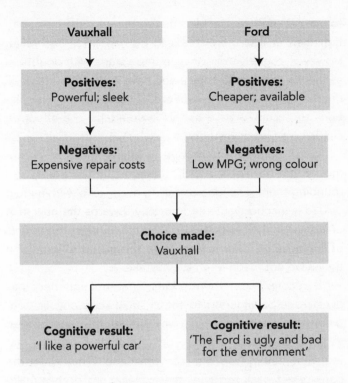

purchase of the Vauxhall the person might begin to worry that perhaps they made the wrong choice. They begin to recall the positives of the one they rejected (i.e. the Ford) and the negatives of the one they chose! This can lead to unhappiness, misery and even attempts to reverse their choice.

In divorces where another individual has come between you and a previous love object the same mechanism tends to occur. When it is decided that a divorce is the best solution then at first there tends to be happiness and relief. However, cognitive dissonance often starts with doubts as to the wisdom of the choice you have made. It is not at all unusual for multiple separations, divorces and reconciliations to occur. As hard as this is on adults, the effect on children can be devastating.

When parents divorce due to affairs, the children are most often bewildered and frightened by the events surrounding them. The idea of 'falling out of love' with a mum or dad is inconceivable and hostility towards the new man or woman in their lives is likely. This can enhance the effects of cognitive dissonance and cause the parent to wonder if they have not made a terrible mistake.

If reconciliation then occurs, the situation becomes even more bewildering to the child. Usually one or both parents have tried to explain why they left their spouse with vague explanations such as 'being unhappy' and the fact that they 'fell in love with someone else'. Thus when the parents get back together the explanations do not make sense to the children.

This does not mean that parents should always remain together, regardless of their feelings, 'for the sake of the children'. People need to get on with their lives. Mistaken marriages and relationships occur. However, when a divorce happens each parent must consider their explanations carefully and keep in mind the possibility of a reconciliation with the estranged partner. Working with the other parent to come up with a satisfactory explanation for the children is in everybody's interest. Both parents should jointly decide on what they will and will not tell the children. After this is done then they should meet together with the children to explain the new state of affairs.

The explanations given should emphasize that the separation is not due to the actions of the children but has instead come from inside the adults involved. Any attempts to use the children to manipulate, berate, humiliate or chastise one parent or the other should stringently be avoided. The content of what is told to the children should be written down and kept by both parents. In this way, when the children inevitably ask again in the years to come why the parents divorced, they can refer back to the agreed 'script' and give consistent answers.

Loss of love

If a divorce occurs due to a loss of love or affection for the other partner, there is a genuine danger that children will fear that a mum or dad will stop loving them. Adults can clearly distinguish between an unceasing love for a child and a changeable love for another adult. Children generally cannot. Thus this topic needs to be addressed repeatedly as the child grows and their ability to reason matures. If this is ignored then insecurities and fears, often displayed through destructive behaviour, become likely.

Abuse or neglect

When the reason for the divorce is physical/emotional abuse or neglect, any children involved may initially feel a great sense of relief that the fighting and arguing has stopped. This feeling of well-being is often then followed by a sense of guilt. Children can enjoy the absence of tension and fear in the household but at the same time believe that somehow they have betrayed one parent or the other by wishing that they were apart. Discussions by both parents addressing this issue are needed. The emphasis again needs to be that it is not the child's fault that the parents have separated. Children need to be reassured that there is nothing they can do now (or could have done in the past) that will keep the parents together.

Addiction

When a divorce occurs due to an addiction by one or both partners, it is typical for children to believe that 'if only the drinking (or porn, drugs, etc.) stops, mum and dad will get back together.' While this occasionally happens, it tends to be rare. As a responsible parent you need to assess carefully whether this is a reality or not, and then talk with your son or daughter openly and truthfully about it. If the damage to your feelings and relationship is too severe, the children need to know that reconciliation is not going to happen, no matter what changes either partner makes.

A bid for freedom

Perhaps the hardest type of divorce to explain to children is where the parents have decided to go their separate ways due to a desire to 'be free', pursue a lost career, or simply because they have grown tired of their mate. There is nothing really concrete that parents can point to in explaining their reasons for separating. Thus children tend to be left in a state of anxiety or dread where they are afraid of 'something' but nobody can really explain to them what it is.

Parents have sometimes manufactured reasons for a divorce to pacify their children's worries but this is very difficult to maintain over time and can lead to children losing trust in your truthfulness in other areas. The old saying that 'honesty is the best policy' is usually right. If you do not know the real reason for the divorce, try telling the children what you do know and feel. It is okay to admit to the kids that you are not totally clear on why you have to leave their mum or dad. However, again you need to clarify that this does not mean that you will grow tired of *them* in the same way.

In all of the situations where a relationship ends in separation or divorce, consideration needs to be given to the children's future and how the parents will cooperate on childrearing. Remember that you are the parents to your offspring for their entire lives. When a couple separates, they are still bound by the tie of having had a child together. The sooner both parties accept this simple truth the better.

Rather than argue about discipline techniques, allowed activities and ages of consent it is much more productive to establish a simple rule between the parents from the start. This rule is stated as 'two yeses are a yes; two nos are a no; and one yes and one no are a no.'

- If both parents agree that a child can do an activity (two yeses) then the child gets to do it.

- If both parents say no then the child is prohibited from doing it.

- If one parent says yes and one says no, the child cannot do the activity.

Mum's response	Dad's response	Parental response
Yes	Yes	Yes
Yes	No	No
No	Yes	No
No	No	No

Suppose for example your teen wants a tattoo of her boyfriend's name on her arm. One parent might believe that this is a good idea and feels that granting the request will win the daughter's favour. The other parent might find the idea abhorrent. Rather than promise the daughter anything, or dump the responsibility for the decision on the other parent, a stock response should be to say they will talk with the other parent about it. Since one parent says yes and one says no, *both* parents tell the girl that she cannot have the tattoo.

In this manner the parents continue as a united front for important decisions about their child. This does not grant one parent control over the other, for the boot will invariably be on the other foot at some point in the future (i.e. the first parent wants to refuse the request while the second would be happy to agree to it). This arrangement helps parents remain involved in the life of their son or daughter and maintains a sense of stability and continuity for the child.

17. Mirror, Mirror, on the Wall

Have you ever known anybody who wanted to become fat? By this I mean not the person who wants to return to a 'healthy' body weight after a severe illness or a procedure such as chemotherapy, but someone who decides they want to be grossly, obscenely fat. What would your reaction be if a mate of yours, or somebody you loved, came up and said 'I've decided to eat nothing but bangers and mash until I weigh at least 20 stone'? Most people would be totally gobsmacked and not know what to say or do.

In this hypothetical situation, almost everyone would begin by questioning the origins of such a desire. We would wonder about our friend's sanity and reasoning ability. Then we would most likely encourage a consultation with a counsellor. We might try to talk them out of the desire but rarely would we try tactics such as bargaining with them about how much or what to eat. It is highly unlikely that we would accept such a goal at face value.

Such a situation is posited simply to stimulate consideration of a situation where a family member comes to us with the polar opposite desire that they wish to lose weight. If someone expresses such a desire, most people respond with encouragement. Our society has long glorified being thin. Simply look at any magazine featuring 'the glamorous people' and it would be hard to find an issue that does not talk about the weight loss of this or that movie star, rock star or model.

THINK ABOUT IT

With our children we tend to accept their statements that they want to lose weight as being a good or at least acceptable idea without questioning their motives. Eating disorders tend to start with such statements. It is true that most attempts to lose weight are innocent expressions. However, it is the situation where the child becomes obsessed with losing weight that is of concern here.

When a youngster, usually but not always an adolescent, wants to have a flatter stomach or better-looking figure we need to talk with them about why:

- Are they jealous of a rival?

- Do they feel that being thin will make them more popular?

- Has somebody made fun of the way they look?

- What is it about their bodies that they do not like, or even hate?

- Are their actions designed to garner praise and status from others?

We might also ask them:

• How much weight do they intend to lose?

• How will they maintain their goal when it is reached?

Only after such questions are answered should we give parental approval for the activity of losing weight. If we help our children to explore such concerns before a programme of weight loss is undertaken, much heartache can be avoided. Consultations with a doctor or nutritionist are well worth the effort before starting.

REMEMBER THIS!!! Eating disorders are one of the emotional problem areas where deaths can and do occur. Roxanne Dryden-Edwards, in a very thorough recent review of the field, suggests that up to 6 per cent of patients with eating disorders die from the condition or associated complications. Eating disorders involve simply stopping eating (anorexia) or something known as the binge-purge syndrome (bulimia). In both situations it is the *process* of losing weight, or an abhorrence of gaining weight, that is the focus of the person's efforts. It is not the goal of 'looking better' that most people assume.

Consider the teenage girl surrounded by images of ultra-thin women who are adored as having the ideal feminine figure. The typical diet and exercise routine of most households does not encourage the development of such a body shape. Therefore in order to become more attractive, your daughter decides to lose some weight. This goal seems harmless enough to most parents and typically they will encourage her to do so without exploring her motives.

By restricting her food intake or skipping meals she is successful at first in losing a few pounds. Peers and her parents tend to remark on how good she looks. This encourages her to continue losing weight. Inevitably she reaches one of the plateaus that all people on diets experience. Now she is presented with a very frustrating conundrum: she wants to continue to obtain the praise of her friends and parents but activities that were successful in the past, such as avoiding snacks and fatty foods, no longer result in weight loss.

Your adolescent now has a very difficult choice: return to her more normal eating pattern, which will probably result in weight gain, or turn to more desperate action. (Maintaining her new eating habits and recently achieved reduced weight is rarely an option, for most efforts by teenagers are by their very nature temporary.) If the more desperate route to continued weight loss is chosen then there are a whole host of potentially devastating activities that she can learn about easily from the media, her friends and the internet. These include:

- Over-the-counter pills to suppress appetite.

- Laxatives.

- Drugs that will stimulate her metabolic rate to burn calories faster.

- Self-induced vomiting.

- Excessive exercise routines.

All of these will lead to the resumption of a rapid (and inherently unsustainable) rate of weight loss.

In most adults these activities tend to be self-limiting. A disgust at vomiting after each meal or ingesting a laxative typically causes us to stop them after a relatively short trial. However, the underdeveloped mind of the teenager can see something almost noble in the pain and discomfort experienced. When this is combined with the resumption of losing weight rapidly and the praise of others for their new look, the result can be deadly.

As the adolescent loses weight she (about 75 per cent of people with eating disorders are female) becomes obsessed with the action instead of the result. Many teens fail to perceive that they have passed a point where others think of them as being underweight. Instead they will have a disturbed body image where they will always see 'fat' in some part of their body when they look in the mirror.

At some point in this process, parents usually become alarmed and try at first to reason with their child. They will say how much better she looked when she was a few pounds heavier. However, such messages fly in the face of their previous statements, the experiences of the adolescent and the media messages teenagers are exposed to daily.

The next step is usually one of negotiation. Parents will allow some activities they would usually prohibit if only their child will eat 'a healthy meal' or item. This bargaining activity ignores the unfortunate reality for the teenager. She sees this as an attempt to either 'make me fat' or else deprive her of a glamorous life. Thus any 'cheating' on her part of the bargain is felt to be justified by a higher moral goal.

There are many other possible routes to the development of anorexia or bulimia. Some causes include:

- Personality disorders.

- Conflict with parents.

- Sexual abuse or other trauma.

- Primary psychiatric disorders such as depression.

Therapists have found that working with teenagers who have anorexia or bulimia can be very prolonged and frustrating. Changing an entrenched disturbed body image is very difficult. The family almost always has to be involved to create the perception that parents are 'on their side' and to help adolescents understand that the problem is not simply one of altering their appearance, changing their calorie intake or moderating the amount of exercise allowed.

One of the most successful approaches to treating eating disorders is that developed by Christopher Dare and his colleagues at the Maudsley Hospital in London in 1985 and known as the Maudsley Model. The key concepts to this model are the inclusion of the family members as active participants in addressing the eating disorder, along with viewing the disorder as a problem outside of the adolescent. In this way the adolescent is not viewed as being 'badly behaved' but instead as part of the family, addressing a condition that is oppressing everyone. Together the family and the therapist, over the course of about a year, work on increasing the adolescent's weight and then giving them back control of their life.

Research studies have yielded empirical support of the efficacy of the Maudsley Model approach in helping families afflicted by this problem, finding a success rate of 80 to 90 per cent. Overcoming an eating disorder is entirely possible when you understand the origins of it and work jointly with the adolescent in a well-thought out approach.

18. Gone Forever

Losses can take many forms:

- Relationships dissolve.

- Redundancy occurs at a job we enjoy.

- Homes can be repossessed.

- Friends move away.

- A loved one is dying or has passed away.

The list goes on and is as extensive as the number of things and people to which it is possible to become attached. Coping with the feelings and insecurities that result is difficult. However, it is something we can all do if we approach the situation with some insight into the mechanisms of loss.

There are many ways in which one can attempt to understand emotional reactions to a loss. Theories have been advanced ranging from social psychology to individually based grieving processes. All have their champions and have been of benefit to many people.

One of the most widely accepted models is that developed by Elisabeth Kübler-Ross who proposed five stages of grief that occur when people experience a loss:

- **Denial.** 'He really doesn't mean it when he says he is leaving me.' 'I can't be dying! The diagnosis must be wrong.'

- **Anger.** 'I hate her for destroying our family by leaving!' 'How dare he die and leave me with the children to raise by myself!'

- **Negotiation.** 'I am sure that we can sort this out and keep the family together.' 'If I pray hard enough, miracles can happen and all will be well.'

- **Depression.** 'It is hopeless and I will never smile again.' 'I just cannot go on without my best friend in life.'

- **Acceptance.** 'Life can go on.' 'I will miss her but I must continue to live for the loved ones I have left.'

These ideas can be beneficial in understanding the reactions of adults and children but require some contemplation in order to avoid the mistakes that many people make when a loss occurs.

It is important to remember that people are not machines. We do not all grieve in the same way or at the same rate. The five stages Kübler-Ross proposed may or may not happen in the order listed. Many people skip one or more of the stages without any enduring difficulty. Many more, especially children, move from one stage to another and then back again several times. All of this is normal when we are trying to cope with loss and does not indicate abnormality or mental illness.

The situation is difficult enough if you are single or part of a couple but when there is a child the process becomes more complex due to having to cope with your child's sadness as well as your own.

Children experience loss as intensely as adults. If you are hurting then it is quite probable that your child is too. If you have to move home due to a job change, for example, your youngster will also suffer the loss of friends, stability and routine. He or she can eventually adjust to all of these, just as you will. However, there are specific things you can do to make the process easier.

Let us suppose that your job has been made redundant and now you must move to a new town. Upon first hearing the news you might respond with 'It must be a mistake!' followed shortly thereafter by anger.

It is important to consider how you would want people to behave towards you in such circumstances, and apply these lessons to your child. Most people would welcome the opportunity to talk about the situation with others. We would not expect the other person to either 'fix' or belittle the problem but simply to listen sympathetically to our distress. We might want helpful suggestions such as pointing out skills that we have forgotten or benefits we might have overlooked.

REMEMBER THIS!!! When we are emotionally hurting we desperately wish for the negative feelings to go away. Unfortunately depression seems to be a necessary part of almost every loss. This serves to stimulate us to eventually find ways of overcoming our sadness. Thus others who try to 'cheer us up' are inadvertently doing the opposite of what we require to resolve our grief.

A question often raised is how much information to give children about the causes of a loss or death. For example, suppose that your spouse has lost his or her job due to chronic alcohol abuse. What should you tell your child?

Throughout my career of helping families I have found that honesty is indeed the best policy. But there is a difference between being 'honest' and being 'brutally honest' and condemning the other person or their actions. You should tell your child enough to satisfy their questions without giving in to the temptation to lecture on morality and behaviour.

Consider a situation where a friend of your child has committed suicide. Parents are tempted with several options:

- Give your child an evasive 'story' such as 'The Lord called him home and we cannot question the ways of God.'

- Lie and say he died of 'natural causes'.

- Use the death as an example to teach a moral lesson to your child. In doing this you might say something like 'See how selfish and wrong it is when a person commits suicide? Look at all the tears and anguish caused by his hanging! You must never do anything like that!'

These responses basically ignore the concerns and feelings of your child – they only assist in evading the discomfort you are experiencing associated with trying to explain why a person decided to take his own life. However, an exploration of causes is exactly what your child requires to help resolve their grief.

Once again, it is not necessary to know the answers to all problems. Telling your child that you don't know why their friend killed himself or why a parent abuses alcohol is perfectly acceptable when it is the truth. This will be recognized for what it is and in turn creates the opportunity for a search for solutions *together*. You will then be able to talk openly about fears, poor choices and desperate acts. This can lead to a discussion of alternative actions the friend or parent could have taken, such as talking with their friends, counsellors and parents. All ideas should be openly examined. Engaging in this sort of dialogue is the most valuable course of action you as a parent can take.

Epilogue

I have always enjoyed the challenge of working with families, for despite the similarities of their problems it seems that there are always things that I have never before encountered. I am constantly learning from the people with whom I work and I have every expectation that this shall continue for the rest of my professional life.

From this I have come to the modest insight that there is no such thing as the only or best way of working to solve difficulties. The number of possible approaches is almost limitless. I have tried to cover as many approaches as possible in this book without making it too tedious. Certainly there are other activities that I might be judged as having overlooked, and for that I apologize. The ones that I have included are those I have come across in my 42 years of clinical experience, in the work of other professionals or in the research that I try to review as often as possible. All of them have passed the test of practical application in my experience.

Parenting is indeed a challenge but it can also be the most rewarding of life's activities. There is nothing I know of that can compare to the experience of watching your child walk across that college stage, or take the hand of a soulmate and say 'I do', and start their own life's voyage.

Despite all the costs, both emotional and financial, I would start my own family all over again if offered the chance, without even blinking an eye. It is this attitude that I would hope that you take with you. All of life's problems are solvable. The ultimate adventure awaits you and being a parent is worth it all.

Sources

American Association of Open Adoption Agencies, www.openadoption.org

Atherton, J.S., *Learning and Teaching: Piaget's developmental theory*, www.learningandteaching.info/learning/piaget.htm

Barker, Phil, 'Cognitive Dissonance', *Beyond Intractability*, eds. Guy Burgess and Heidi Burgess. Conflict Information Consortium, University of Colorado, Boulder. Posted September 2003. www.beyondintractability.org.bi-essay.cognitive-dissonance

Beck, H.P., 'General Psychology', www1.appstate.edu/~beckhp/bellandpad.htm

Changing Minds, http://changingminds.org/explanations/needs/maslow.htm

CSOM Publications-Recidivism of Sexual Offenders, www.csom.org/pubs/recidsexof.html

Dryden-Edwards, Roxanne, MD, www.medicinenet.com/anorexia_nervosa

Elisabeth Kübler-Ross Foundation, www.ekrfoundation.org/five-stages-of-grief

Fremont, Wanda P., MD, 'School Refusal in Children and Adolescents', *American Family Physician*, vol. 68, no. 8, pp. 1555–1561, 2003 Oct 15

Infinite Innovations Ltd, www.brainstorming.co.uk

Johnson, A.M., Falstein, E.I., Szurek, S.A., Svendsen, M., 'School phobia', *American Journal of Orthopsychiatry* (1941) vol. 11, pp. 702–711

Kerr, Patrick L., Muehlenkamp, Jennifer J., Turner, James M., 'Nonsuicidal Self-Injury: A Review of Current Research for Family Medicine and Primary Care Physicians', *The Journal of the American Board of Family Medicine*, vol. 23, no. 2 (March–April 2010), pp. 240–259

Office for National Statistics, www.ons.gov.uk

Oxford Brookes University, www.brookes.ac.uk

McLeod, S.A. (2007), 'Skinner – Operant Conditioning', www.simplypsychology.org/operant-conditioning.html

Medlin, Nadine Marie, 'Adolescent Psychological Separation-Individuation and the Identity Formation Process' (1 January 1991), *ETD collection for University of Nebraska-Lincoln*, http://digitalcommons.unl.edu/dissertations/AAI9133306

Resnick, Michael D., et al., 'Protecting Adolescents from Harm: Findings from the National Longitudinal Study on

Adolescent Health', *Journal of the American Medical Association* 278, no. 10 (1997), pp. 823–832

NHS Choices, www.nhs.uk/Conditions/Bedwetting/Pages/Treatment.aspx

Rice, Keith E., www.integratedsociopsychology.net

Rhodes, Paul, 'The Maudsley Model of Family Therapy for Children and Adolescents with Anorexia Nervosa: Theory, Clinical Practice, and Empirical Support', *Australia and New Zealand Journal of Family Therapy*, vol. 24, no. 4 (2003), pp. 191–198

Truax, Charles B. and Carkhuff, Robert R., *Toward Effective Counseling and Psychotherapy: Training and Practice*, Aldine Pub. Co., Chicago

University of South Alabama, www.southalabama.edu

US National Library of Medicine, www.ncbi.nlm.nih.gov/pubmedhealth/PMH0002518

Watson, Emily, www.muskingum.edu/~psych/psycweb/history/watson.htm

Index